SYSTEMIC COACHING

SYSTEMIC COACHING

DIFFERENTIATE YOUR COACHING FOR EXCEPTIONAL RESULTS

Ichak K. Adizes, Ph.D.

Edition 2023

PUBLICATIONS

Adizes Institute Publications

© 2023 Dr. Ichak K. Adizes
books@adizes.com
Website: https://.adizesbooks.com

All rights reserved. No part of this publication may be reproduced in any form, by any means (including electronic, photocopying, recording or otherwise), without permission of the author and the publisher.

Adizes® is a registered trademark of Ichak Adizes, LLC.

Symbergetic™ is a trademark of Ichak Adizes, LLC.

Published by Adizes Institute Publications
Carpinteria, CA 93013

2023 Edition

ISBN: 978-1-952587-06-1

Library of Congress Control Number has been applied for.

Printed in the United States of America

Contents

Acknowledgments   *xiii*
Foreword   *xv*
Introduction   *xvii*

Part 1
Coaching and the Adizes Methodology   23

What is coaching?   23
Levels of change produced by coaching   24
    First-order change   24
    Second-order change   25
How is coaching different from other disciplines?   26
What is the Adizes Methodology?   28
Coaching with Adizes: What are the benefits? How is Adizes different from other methodologies?   29

Part 2:
The Adizes Foundational tools and their application to personal life   33

Foundational Tool #1:
Understanding the individual as a system   35
    Growing the Adizes way   37

Foundational Tool #2:
PAEI (the four building blocks for a healthy life)   41
    The incompatibility of the four PAEI roles   59
    PAEI as a code for personality style   62
    The perfect person does not and cannot exist (but that does not prohibit you from working on yourself!)   66
    How we make decisions: the four voices in our head   69
    The sequence of decision-making and the five imperatives   72

Foundational Tool #3:
The 8 Step Decision-Making Process   77

Foundational Tool #4:
The lens through which you see the world (perceptions of reality)   89
    How each PAEI style perceives reality   94

Foundational Tool #5:
The lifecycle of the individual   97
    The Growing Stages   100
    The Aging Stages   113

Part 3:
Self-coaching — "First, grow yourself" — The Adizes Systemic Coaching Framework   **119**

Adizes for First-Order of Change   120

   Self-diagnosis for first-order change: Defining potential improvement points (PIPs)   120

   Self-coaching protocol for first-order change   122

Adizes for Second-Order Change   126

   Self-diagnosis for second-order change   126

   SPIRAL DYNAMICS: What are your values?   134

   Step 1: Arresting the manifestations in column 6   159

   Step 2: Work on relieving the PIPs in column 4/5   161

   Step 3: Work on solving the PIPs in columns 2 and 3   162

   Step 4: Releasing column 1   165

   Step 5: Finding a solution with the four PAEI imperatives   169

   Step 6: Implementing   171

Part 4:
How to coach others with Adizes   **183**

   Traditional coaching approaches: the one-size-fits-all trap   183

   Before you coach others, you must discover your own coaching personality.   185

   Benefits vs. blind spots of each style in coaching   186

   And one more thing before you go and coach: remember to switch to listening mode.   190

How to coach the different PAEI styles   192

How to coach the (P) style	193
How to coach the (A) style	201
How to coach the (E) style	210
How to coach the (I) style	221

Part 5:
For certified coaches of other approaches — 227

Epilogue — *231*
About the Author — *235*

Acknowledgments

I want to thank Yechezkel Madanes for his invaluable contributions to this book. Yechezkel organized my lecture notes, interviewed me, and helped me to structure and produce the Adizes theory parts of the book. How it applies to coaching I owe him a debt. He is a certified coach of some great repute and without his contribution this book would not have seen the light of day. Thank you, Yechezkel.

Thank you, also, to Olga Gurskaya whose valuable comments improved the book.

Foreword

In my work as a coach, I have always been fascinated by the complexity of human beings. One way this complexity manifests is how, in the same situation, different people react completely differently. This is a key insight for coaches: people think, feel, and act differently, so we cannot approach our coachees as if they were the same. Generic approaches fail. What works with one coachee may not work with another.

Driven by Thomas Leonard's passion, the International Association of Coaching has dedicated the last two decades to finding out the distinctive features of a masterful coach. I've been privileged to serve at the IAC, and I deeply believe understanding your coachee's unique vision of life is the foundation of a masterful coaching session. It allows you to tailor coaching to what a coachee truly needs.

The rich interrelationships between the coaching masteries express themselves in a multiplicity of ways. In order to unlock a coachee's endless potential, you must create an environment of trust, enter a state of presence, and view the world from your coachee's perspective.

In *Systemic Coaching*, Dr. Adizes lays out a variety of tools that enable you to do that. You will not only understand the depth of your coachee's personality, but – as you draw from the Adizes Methodology tools – you will understand the lenses through which they see the world; which stage of the lifecycle they inhabit; the limiting beliefs that may be holding them back; how different people make and take decisions; and many other tools critical for coaching others.

When I first learned about the Adizes Methodology, I was amazed by its vastness and ability to deal with both simple and complex organizational issues. In this book, you will see how the Methodology translates into a system for coaching individuals, helping them to solve both simple and complex issues (first and second order change, respectively). Whether you learn the Adizes Methodology as supplemental to your existing coaching practice, or you certify as an Adizes Systemic Coach, these tools will be of great value. They will put you on your own path towards masterful coaching and living.

I want to emphasize "living," as this book contains a complete section on how to coach yourself. A tenet of the IAC is that you must "live the coaching masteries." Dr. Adizes teaches us that before we can coach others, we must be able to grow ourselves.

What intrigued me the most about Systemic Coaching is how Dr. Adizes, with his signature wit and wisdom, weaves together the tools, the coaching, and the foundational information we all need.

Whether you are a new or seasoned coach, a helping professional, or a manager or CEO looking to empower colleagues, follow the guidelines and carefully learn to use the tools in this book.

I hope that you will be as inspired and excited as I am by the applicability and depth of this life-changing methodology. Not only will you better coach others, but you'll grow and become wiser in every area of your life.

Jose Manuel Del Rio Zamacona
President, International Association of Coaching, *2018-2021*

Introduction

It's well known that we are living in a time of accelerated change. Everybody can feel it, in every area of life. And these times put stress on all of us—in other words, where there is change, there are problems.

And what do you need to do when you have problems? You need to manage them, because problems created by change, that are not attended to, can soon become crises. Figuring out how to manage problems created by change has been and continues to be my passion for almost fifty years.

And I've seen change. In my autobiography[1] I go over the story of my life, including my decades-long career as a management professor and organizational therapist. As someone who was born in the first half of the 20th century, I've seen massive amounts of change. From geographical change—Yugoslavia, the country I was born in, is a country that doesn't exist anymore—to economic, political, social, and even environmental. In less than one hundred years, the world has changed more than in all previous generations. And as said, where there are

---

1. Adizes, I.: *The Accordion Player. A Memoir*, forthcoming, Adizes Institute Publications, Santa Barbara: CA

changes there are problems. Just open any newspaper today and you'll see what I mean.

I was always fascinated by the field of management and so I studied, graduated, and later became a professor in this area—developing a proprietary methodology for organizational therapy. Based on feedback from my clients, I have concluded that my methodology is not only applicable to organizations, governments, and families, but to individuals as well. The Adizes Methodology, as it applies to companies, is well covered in over twenty-six books and translated to thirty-six languages. There is also a book on how to apply the methodology to marriage and family.2 In this book I will cover how to apply the Adizes Methodology to achieve individual growth.

Leadership starts with *self-leadership*, your ability to know and manage yourself—so you can be a healthy, well-rounded person and have your act together. It's only from a foundation of inner strength that you can become successful in your life. And it's only from that point of internal wholeness, by developing the necessary self-trust and self-respect, that you can then integrate yourself externally in the world.

And why is this so?

The field of physics teaches us that, at any point in time, energy is fixed. And we indeed see that even the most productive human being has only twenty-four hours in a day. What I have learned is that in each one of us, that fixed energy gets predictably allocated. First, it is used to solve our inner conflicts, our internal struggles. Then, the surplus, if any, is used to achieve our personal and professional goals.

Internal problems can consume you. They can drain most of your vital energy. I've seen it happen countless times throughout my career. Show me a person who is going through a personal crisis and I'll show

---

2. Adizes, I.: (2015) *The Power of Opposites. How to Succeed in Your Marriage and Family Not in Spite of, But Because of Your Differences*, Adizes Institute Publications, Santa Barbara: CA. Available in multiple languages at https://publications.adizes.com

you someone who's spending (at least for some part of each day), their own fixed energy to solve an inner turmoil, with little leftover for family and even less for a career. …Disintegration is a sign of disease. Integration is a sign of health. When we are worried, we say, "This guy/family/company/country is falling apart." When we are impressed, we say, "He/she/they have it all together …"

Let me give you another example: Take a human being who went to the best business school, got an MBA with all As, and inherited a hundred million dollars from his parents. Good education, lots of money, and let's just throw in for good measure, very good looking. Is he going to be successful? You may be tempted to say, "Of course! This guy has the money, the looks, and the education!" But what if I were to tell you that, for whatever reason, he has no self-respect and no self-trust? With sufficient sacrifice, almost anyone can get through school and get high grades. Relatively speaking, this is not so hard to achieve. But to develop your inner strength is not so easy. If a person is, emotionally, full of unsolved issues (e.g., not knowing the right thing to do, troubled over what others think of him or her, not knowing where he or she is heading), how successful is this person going to be? Not very, because *most of his energy is being wasted between his ears.* He is stuck in the inner chatter of his own mind. The hundred million dollars in the bank is like having a Ferrari but not having the key to turn it on.

What is the biggest asset of a company for sustainable success? It's not how big or strong they are in the marketplace. It's not how much cash they have. It's not how many protected patents they possess. It's their culture. It's how internally integrated they are, because this is what will allow them to handle change without falling apart—and change must be handled or else you die in the marketplace. In the same way, your biggest asset is not your money, your education, or your looks. It's your mindset. Your mindset will reveal how integrally integrated you are as a human being. Mindset is for an individual what culture is to a company.

In this book my aim is to give you self-coaching and self-management tools that will help you develop a healthy, systemic mindset that, in turn, will minimize your own internal disintegration. From this internal foundation, you will find the energy to coach others.

I am inviting you on a fascinating journey, during which we will look at human beings through the prism of the management methodology I have worked on and tested for over fifty years. The coaching principles within it won't solve all of your issues, and it's not intended to replace psychotherapy. Sometimes the noise between our ears does require professional intervention. But it will definitely challenge you to look at life and the problems created by change in an innovative way. Our problems are becoming increasingly systemic and therefore require systemic solutions. And the very same framework that I use to coach my clients can also be used to coach yours. It will give you the tools you need to help yourself and others grow. It will present a methodology how to approach and solve your challenges in a systemic and organized way—looking at the totality, the system that you are— so that you and your coachees can conserve as much energy as possible and use that energy to advance life goals.

HOW THIS BOOK IS ORGANIZED

Parts 1 and 2 present the foundations of the Adizes Methodology and its benefits for coaching.

In Part 3 ("First, Grow Yourself"), we will dive into a self-coaching framework based on Adizes tools: to provide a comprehensive diagnosis of your problems, techniques for effective decision-making and structured problem-solving, and efficient implementation of solutions. It is necessary to learn and apply this framework inward, because before you can coach others you must first successfully coach yourself.

In Part 4, "How to Coach Others With Adizes," we will discover how the methodology can be used to coach people.

And Part 5, "For Certified Coaches of Other Approaches," it will show you how you can benefit from incorporating Adizes tools into your existing coaching tool kit.

My hope is that this book will equip you with the valuable tools you'll need to face the challenges associated with these times of rapidly accelerated change—and thrive right through them—as you turn life's setbacks into growth opportunities.

Just thinking,
Ichak Kalderon Adizes

Part 1

Coaching and the Adizes Methodology

WHAT IS COACHING?

Coaching is a process designed to help another person set and achieve their personal and professional goals, by creating awareness and responsibility through questioning and conversation. The recipient is encouraged to stretch and take responsibility for his or her own development, to discover new possibilities and solutions, and to take action with support from the coach.

In recent decades, coaching has become a great tool for helping nonclinical populations develop and achieve personal and professional goals.

Coaching is often described as a way of helping people get from where they are today (Point A) to where they want to be (Point B). In order to help their clients begin the process of moving toward their goals, coaches use a range of communication techniques (such as engaged listening, questioning, and clarifying) to help their "coachees" experience a shift in perspective, discover new ways to take action, and realize that they are capable of achieving their goals.[1]

LEVELS OF CHANGE PRODUCED BY COACHING[2]

FIRST-ORDER CHANGE

Often clients seek coaching because they want to achieve a specific short-term goal.

A person who is undecided about a career decision may seek coaching to get clarity and explore his options. Perhaps only one, or a few, coaching conversations will be sufficient for such a purpose. The coach will shed light on the different options, help the client see the pros and cons of each, and support the action the client chooses to take.

In another example, an individual who cannot overcome chronic lateness may want to learn some techniques for better time management. A coaching process aimed at building the habit of promptness may help her with that goal.

In both cases, however, the coaching is said to produce first-order change, as it's only aimed at generating external behavioral changes and new skill acquisition. Although the person is acquiring a new skill and producing the desired behavioral change, they are not really being transformed. These coachees will continue to view the world

---

1. Cox, Elaine (2013), *Coaching Understood: A Pragmatic Inquiry into the Coaching Process*, Los Angeles; London: Sage Publications
2. See Bast, M. and Thomson C. (2005), *Out of the Box Coaching*, Louisburg, KA: Ninestar Publishing.

through the same lenses, and with the same worldview, as before the coaching.

SECOND-ORDER CHANGE

Second-order change takes place when coaching challenges the person to examine the lens through which they assign meaning and interpret reality. Perhaps the coachee who is always late will discover that she values freedom to a degree that inhibits her ability to be on time, something she perceives as restrictive. Inadvertently, she may see arriving to meetings on time as being submissive, and therefore a threat to her independence. She makes people wait for her, although this causes her relationships to suffer. Through coaching, this person may begin to uncover her limiting beliefs and explore her own identity and values. This coachee may then realize that she can be a freedom-loving person while simultaneously being respectful of other peoples' time. She may finally discover that these two states of being (being free and being on time) are not incompatible—they actually *can coexist*.

When this kind of breakthrough happens, there is a before-and-after effect. There is a shift in the person's point of view, and their habitual way of reacting comes into question. From this point forward, even if the repetitive behavior comes up, the person will experience it differently because they have now developed an observing self that recognizes the unproductive pattern.

Second-order change typically involves a complete coaching process, because although an illumination can occur in a single coaching session, the breaking of old habits and the cultivation of new, healthier ones often requires some time. Masterful coaches will skillfully support their clients through the ups and downs of such a process.

The Adizes Methodology provides tools that allow coaches to analyze when a first- or a second-order change is called for, and what reasonable expectations are required to achieve success.

HOW IS COACHING DIFFERENT FROM OTHER DISCIPLINES?

Unlike mentoring, therapy, consulting and teaching, the discipline of coaching is distinctive **because it proceeds through a learner-led exploration** to build capacity, skills, and competencies.

In *consulting*, the consultant is the expert who advises clients on what to do and how to solve a specific challenge.

In *mentoring*, a mentee learns and gains knowledge from a mentor's experience.

In teaching, there is a one-way transfer of knowledge.

People often seek *therapy* when a problem reaches crisis mode. Therapy focuses on exploring in-depth emotional issues that cannot be solved by coaching. Common signs that a person is not coachable and may need therapy are: a lack of cooperation with the coaching process; poor follow up and implementation of decisions made during the process; heavy emotional blockages that impede taking action and responsibility and prevent the coachee from committing fully to the process. In therapy, there are no such expectations and so the process will continue to explore all avenues for healing. In contrast, coaching requires that coachees take full responsibility and be fully committed to the task of stretching and building their own capacity.[3]

---

3. That's why coaching requires that the client is coachable–fully committed to the process and taking responsibility for themselves to solve the problem and challenge at hand. We will expand more on the issue of coachability later in the book.

The following table summarizes the differences across these professions:

	Coaching	Therapy	Mentoring	Consulting	Teaching/Training
Works with …	Healthy, functioning individuals who want to grow and expand their capacity and competency.	Individuals having difficulty coping with daily life, and who want to heal emotional pain.	Individuals who want to grow professionally.	Individuals, teams, and organizations that want to solve specific problems.	Individuals and teams who want to acquire a particular skill.
Type of relationship	Client, or **"coachee," is the expert**. The coach works with the coachee as a partner but is not necessarily an expert in the coachee's field.	Therapist is the expert. The therapist works with a patient as a licensed mental health professional.	Mentor is the expert. The mentor works 1:1 with the mentee as an expert who's higher up in the hierarchy of the mentee's profession and gives them advice.	Consultant is the expert. The consultant works with organizations, teams, and individuals, as an expert in the field to find resolutions for professional problems.	Trainer is the expert. The trainer works as an instructor, as a person skilled in particular abilities that the trainee lacks.
Type of communication	Facilitates learning and empowers coachees to find their own solutions. Challenges coachees to take responsibility and action.	The same like coaching but the therapist has tools to dig deeper into the sources of the dysfunctionality.	Gives advice and recommendations. Shares guidance and insights from personal experience.	Gives advice and recommendations. May or may not help with implementation.	Direct transfer of knowledge.

	Coaching	Therapy	Mentoring	Consulting	Teaching/Training
Orientation and Focus	Future. Personal growth. Helps set achievable goals and build self-awareness and capacity. Works on the person.	Past. Helps resolve past pain and heal traumas. Works on the person.	Present and future roles. Helps the mentee with a current situation and issues. Works on the person.	Future, present and medium-term. Works on a problem to build solutions, systems, structures and processes.	Present and future.
Diagnosis	Coaches assess the coachee's reality, but don't diagnose conditions and disorders.	Therapists diagnose mental-health conditions and disorders.	Mentor may offer a very informal diagnosis, specific to the mentee's needs.	Consultants diagnose a client's situation.	May assess skill gaps.
Duration of relationship	Typically short. From a few sessions to a few months.	Longer process. Sometimes up to several years.	Both short and long.	Both short and long. Engaged to solve a specific issue.	Short.

WHAT IS THE ADIZES METHODOLOGY?

The Adizes Methodology is a systemic methodology that provides organizations with tools to help minimize uncertainty and risk—in order to make better decisions and implement them with minimum loss of energy, promptly, and as decided. This is done by creating and nurturing a culture of mutual trust and respect through ongoing collaborative leadership.

Originated in the early 1970s, the methodology has been continuously refined, tested in the field, and perfected over the last five decades. In recent years more applications of the methodology have appeared—proving its universality—as it applies not only to organizations and governments, but also to families[4] and couples. Which brings us to the subject of this book: Can the methodology be utilized to coach individuals? The answer is yes. Because a person, like a company, is a system. Companies require a culture of mutual trust and respect in order to avoid wasting limited fixed energy on destructive conflicts. The same applies to human beings. Without self-trust and self-respect, humans will waste their energy on conflicts "between their ears," leaving themselves unable to properly cope with the world. And that is what this book is about.

COACHING WITH ADIZES: WHAT ARE THE BENEFITS? HOW IS ADIZES DIFFERENT FROM OTHER METHODOLOGIES?

Let's take a look at some classic coaching tools and strategies. What are some of the things professional coaches typically do?

A professional coach will:

- Create an environment of trust and respect, within which the coachee can open up and feel safe.

- Use the coaching process as a learning experience, and coaching sessions as a learning environment.

- Establish a rapport with every coachee, regardless of the coachee's personality style (in other words, know how to create trust and chemistry with different people).

---

4. Adizes, op.cit, page 16.

- Tailor interventions—to prevent "one-size-fits-all" coaching.
- Challenge limiting beliefs.
- Leverage the coachees' pain as fuel to produce change.
- Empower coachees through strength-based coaching.
- Facilitate the coachees' understanding of the way they view and interpret reality and events.
- Depersonalize problems, with the understanding that problems are contingent to the stage where the person currently is in life.

As a result, a coach will help a coachee to:

- Better understand themselves and the way they operate in the world.
- Explore their own values.
- Set goals.
- Discover their available possibilities and options.
- Develop new skills, capabilities, and competencies.
- See their current performance level, move out of their comfort zone, and realize their potential.
- Create an action plan, then take action to produce measurable results.
- See their own patterns and understand the root causes of their problems.
- Improve their decision-making.
- Improve their emotional intelligence and the quality of their relationships.
- Take responsibility. Connect to and leverage the pain a problem is causing (and will continue to cause), in order to motivate them to take responsibility for themselves and change.

- Connect to their own humanity, learn to set realistic expectations for themselves, and steer away from overly perfect ideals.

How does Adizes help potentiate the above coaching deliverables? Adizes offers a variety of tools that can accelerate the effectiveness and efficiency of coaching. The following tables demonstrate how these tools fulfill key coaching needs and produce results for coachees:

Coaching Need and Goal	Adizes Tools and Concepts
To build trust, and help the coachee to feel truly understood	Methodology of understanding PAEI styles
To foster a continuous learning mindset in the coachee	Integration, mutual trust, and respect
To establish rapport	Creating a sense of mutual trust and respect
To avoid "one-size-fits-all" coaching	Matching your coaching style to your coachee's personality style
To provide strength-based and empowerment coaching	Understanding there is no PAEI person that excels in everything
To help the coachee establish an understanding of their view and interpretation of reality and events	Perceptions of Reality: is/want/should
To depersonalize the coachee's problems, and demonstrate that problems are contingent to the stage where the person currently is in life	Adizes lifecycle of the individual, of the family, and of the organization

Benefit/Result for Coachee	Adizes Tools and Concepts
Learns to navigate a world of continuous change	The Adizes alignment of systems and subsystems
Finds self-understanding and personality awareness	Understanding PAEI styles

Benefit/Result for Coachee	Adizes Tools and Concepts
Learns to evaluate their options	The Adizes Criteria Tables
Realizes their behavior patterns and finds the root causes of their problems	The Attribution Matrix; PAEI missing roles, their self-mismanagement style
Understands their emotional reactions when under stress	PAEI backup behaviors
Identifies their decision-making patterns and understands how the "voice in our head" can falsely influence us	PAEI, the 8 Step Decision-Making Process
Comes to understand why they get along with some people and not others	Understanding the PAEI styles
Improves their emotional intelligence, and the quality of their relationships	The need for complimentary teams on any endeavor
Connects to their own humanity, learns to set realistic expectations of themselves and steer away from overly perfect ideals	The incompatibility of roles

The Adizes Methodology can not only be used as a stand-alone coaching system, its tools can also amplify the power of any coaching system already being used. Think of it as "coaching on steroids."

Let's move on now to Part 2 for an introduction to the Adizes Foundational Tools, along with key concepts to help you grow as a coach and, in turn, help others grow.

Part 2:

The Adizes Foundational tools and their application to personal life

Adizes is a vast methodology that has been researched, developed, and perfected over the course of five decades. This section of the book presents the building blocks of the methodology—in particular, the Adizes frameworks, tools, techniques, and key ideas that you will need to coach yourself and others.

Foundational Tool #1:

Understanding the individual as a system

The world, and everything in it, is a collection of systems. Nature is a system. The economy is a system. Your car is a system. Even you, as a person, are a system.

Within every system, by definition, there is a set of subsystems. Your car is comprised of several subsystems. One day your car is going to break down, because one of its subsystems is going to malfunction. It's not a matter of if it's going to break down, it's just a matter of when.

The reason? The subsystems within your car are aging at varying paces. The alternator, which keeps the battery charged and supplies power to your vehicle's electrical system, may be the last subsystem to fail. The fuel pump, however, may falter within the first few years.

It's a fact, then, that given enough time, the subsystems within any system will begin to fall apart. The separate aspects of a system won't necessarily change together. The subsystems will not change or deteriorate in synchronicity. Some will change faster than others. This will create gaps, and as they occur, these gaps will become manifested into what we call "problems."

> *Problems are manifestations of disintegration, which is caused by change.*

Think of your own body. Are your organs aging at different speeds? If you are a smoker, your lungs will age much faster than the rest of your body. If your heart is strained due to obesity you might die sooner. If you eat poorly your arteries may clog and age faster than your body's other subsystems.

It's normal to have problems because it is normal to have change, and change is synonymous with time. Since time cannot be stopped, change cannot be stopped, and the problem if not treated will get worse, becoming a crisis. As Henry Kissinger once said, "a problem that goes unattended is a crisis in waiting."

Granted, there are problems that are solved in time and without intervention, like a small scratch healing on its own. Not every problem requires intervention. But it is up to you to decide which is which. This book is focused on those problems that do not resolve on their own with time.

So, what are the implications of this for your own personal growth? As stated previously: You—as a person—are a system. And as such you are comprised of subsystems: physical, emotional, spiritual, and mental/logical. While your physical subsystem continues to advance (you grow taller, go through puberty, physically mature), and your mental subsystem may be that of a very rational, intelligent person, your emotional subsystem may get stuck in adolescence—and spiritually, you may not have even been born yet. This lack of synchronicity causes what you might call "problems" in your life. You don't have it together. As psychologists say, "Oneness or illness."

GROWING THE ADIZES WAY

It's best to treat problems proactively (i.e., treat them before they become crises). If we proactively and electively treat our problems, we will have a better result than if we react to those problems. This is why doctors recommend having an annual checkup—even if you feel good. The annual checkup might reveal something you can't feel. You might think everything is OK, but this may really not be so. If an issue is discovered, you and your doctor can fix it. Preventatively. Otherwise, when will you take action? When it really hurts! Unfortunately, some people need to have a small heart attack before they will begin a diet and exercise regimen and quit smoking.

The role of self-coaching is to minimize internal disintegration and it all begins with a good diagnosis of what's falling apart. Once internal disintegration has been minimized, energy can be devoted to external integration.

That's how successful individuals grow sustainably: they devote time to fixing the inside, so they can keep growing. The following diagram illustrates a typical misconception about growth. Many people believe sustainable growth looks like this:

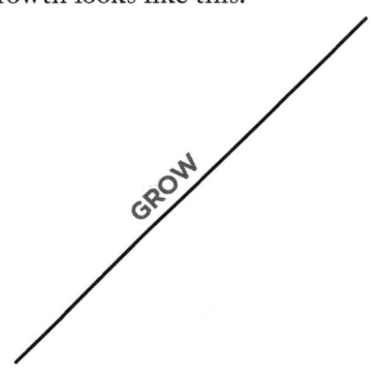

As growth implies change, growth implies disintegration. From time to time, you need to slow down, see what's working/not working, and figure out anything that needs to be done. In other words, you need to reintegrate. And you should not wait until something breaks down to make a diagnosis. Put it on your calendar. It's called maintenance. Everybody needs a maintenance plan. And not just a physical plan, but also mental, emotional, and spiritual plans.

Figure out where improvement is needed. Maybe you need realignment in your health: You work long hours every day which is taking a toll on your body. You career subsystem is improving rapidly, but your health is falling apart. So STOP—create a maintenance plan—devote some time every day to fixing the internal disintegration in your physical subsystem. Out of this diagnosis might come a coaching plan that includes a daily twenty-minute walk on the treadmill.

This perspective is why the Adizes Methodology view of growth looks like this:

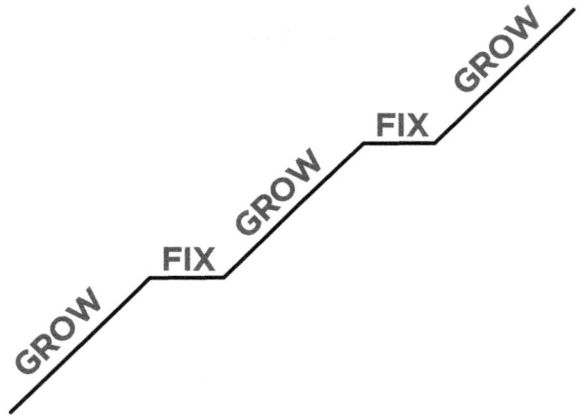

In order to grow sustainably, you should periodically take care of yourself with a maintenance plan. You should detect and fix whatever may be falling apart. You should maintain yourself, because if you maintain yourself well, you will be healthy, and if you are healthy, you will be sustainably successful.

Reintegration by way of rest is done while you sleep, which is why sleep is extremely important for your well-being. Without sleep you are exhausted and cannot function. And the same applies to having a day of rest. The Sabbath (a Sunday or a Friday) is a day off, a day to reintegrate yourself. But that is not enough. You also need to take time and face yourself; find out where you are in need of some fixing. Are you dedicating all of your energy to work and none to your marriage? Do this long enough and we all know where it ends. As one of my clients once said, "One honeymoon is not enough for a lifetime of marriage." Love needs to be maintained and that involves planning, scheduling, and honoring the commitment to meet with your spouse one-on-one—regularly.

Your body needs rest and reintegration, too, and I am not referring only to sleep. I am referring to periodic fasting, which gives your digestive system a chance to rest.

A prescription for failure in life—in your personal life, or marriage, or career—is to take things for granted. Assuming that somehow things will work out without having to do anything.

> *Do not take your health for granted.*
>
> *Do not take love for granted.*
>
> *Do not take your career for granted.*
>
> *Do not take your financial status for granted.*
>
> *Do not take anything for granted.*

The difference between luck and success is that in luck you might like what you get, but in success you have to get what you want. You have to work for it.

We all like to be lucky. The problem is that it is not predictable nor controllable. Relying on luck to be successful, if it happens, will put you to sleep. You will start relying on luck to continue working for you and we all know this does not work. On the contrary, while waiting for luck to be repeated, you might lose in moving forward and will eventually experience failure not in spite of being lucky but because you were lucky.

Many people go the other extreme: spending lots of time with their loved ones, neglecting their professional work, and believing that putting family first means being with one's family constantly. While it may seem like the family subsystem is being attended to, the work subsystem may be falling apart. And ironically, failure in the work subsystem may eventually have a domino effect that carries over into the family subsystem.

To be successful, you cannot take care of one of your subsystems while abandoning the others. You can try, but life will eventually create a crisis in that abandoned realm—to wake you up with a need for balance, and to find that balance you need maintenance.

The more change there is in the external world, the busier we become as we get absorbed by it. The consequence is that we dedicate less and less time to our internal world, and thus we need more and more to work on our reintegration.

It is an unfortunate fact that the modern world, especially in the West, values external successes (i.e., career achievements, and financial wealth), more than the internal achievement of growing as a human being (i.e., staying balanced, and keeping oneself together).

The danger is, as we expend our limited energy to succeed externally, the energy needed for internal integration suffers. It's no surprise that we eventually find ourselves experiencing a nervous breakdown, depression, or anxiety—that is, falling apart.

Foundational Tool #2:

PAEI (the four building blocks for a healthy life)

We have said that an individual, as a whole, is a system. As such, we naturally want to be healthy and have a healthy system.

The question, then, is what makes a system healthy?

To me, a healthy system is one that is effective and efficient, both in the short and the long run. To achieve this, there are four roles that every system requires. I use the acronym PAEI for these four essential roles. Each PAEI role is carried out by a subsystem that uniquely, contributes to the system as a whole. To illustrate their meaning, let's consider each role an organizational vitamin necessary for organizational health.

The PAEI Roles (input)	Makes the System (output)	Time Span
(P)	Effective	Short Run
(A)	Efficient	Short Run
(E)	Effective	Long Run
(I)	Efficient	Long Run

Effectiveness means that the system is able to produce, in practice, the purpose for which it exists. A deodorant is effective if it protects you from odor. A car is effective if it transports you from one place to another. You, as an individual, are effective in the short run if you deliver what is expected of you (meeting your immediate needs, overcoming your day-to-day challenges) via your "doing realm."

In a much bigger sense, it means that you are successfully answering the questions "What am I here for, on this earth? And for whom?" For whom do I exist? For what? Whom am I serving? Who is my "client"?

In our personal lives we have multiple clients that we must provide care for: ourselves, our family, our customers and employers. And for those with a higher level of consciousness add in their country or the planet. Of these clients, who gets priority? Whom do you plan to serve when you wake up in the morning? In a practical sense, this is what drives you to wake up every day and go into the world and work and perform and contribute your unique gifts and talents. You are serving. That is how you carry out the (P role).

To be effective in the long run means that you will be able to keep serving in the future. For instance, you may have found your vocation, a way to serve in the world, through being a life coach. It's what you love doing, it's what uplifts you and gives you energy and causes you to lose track of time, place, everything. If you plan for the future, stay proactive, and keep studying—training yourself and learning new techniques and skills—you will be able to be effective in the long run as a life coach. In a world that changes continuously, if you continuously provide yourself with the skillsets, toolsets, and mindsets that will allow you to keep understanding and helping your clients, then you will make yourself sustainable. That's you carrying out the (E) role which improves your whole for the long run.

Now, let's look at the (A) and (I) roles. In the table above, the (A) and (I) are roles that make the system efficient. Similar to the (P) and (E) roles, (A) makes the system efficient in the short run, while the (I) role makes it more efficient in the long run.

To be efficient means that you are able to perform an action with a minimum of effort and no waste of resources. Think of two different cars, for instance—a Ford Focus and a Honda Civic—each may be effective, because either one can take you 120 miles from LA to San Diego. But the Civic will use less fuel, making it more efficient than the Focus. As a life coach you may be earning good money and doing a great job, but outside of your professional life you might be very disorganized. Perhaps you lose documents, miss phone calls, and waste your time and energy on unnecessary little personal conflicts. All of this will make you inefficient in the short run. In order to stay on top of these things you need to develop your (A) role. Your (A) subsystem will take care of all the logistical needs that your life demands—bill paying, meal planning, calendar scheduling, people juggling, etc. The (A) role will help you to stay efficient. Efficiency in your personal life means having good habits that allow you to establish routines that save you time, money, and energy. An efficient personal life means that all of your short-term needs and obligations have been met, which leaves energy left over to channel into the other areas of your life.

To be efficient in the long run, you need to ensure that all of your subsystems are working in unison—that your physical subsystem is not neglected if you devote energy to your mental subsystem. You expend energy keeping the total system operating, nevertheless. That is why when we are falling apart, we say, "I have no energy." You are constantly tired. You sit in front of your computer trying to work, but your tired body or your troubled emotions demand attention, and guess what? You cannot work. This is where the (I) role comes in. The (I) subsystem's job is to keep all four of your subsystems aligned. Not only internally but also externally: through having friends you love, a family you love, a community you love. The (I) helps you to become wholly "together" so you can be more internally efficient and liberate vital energy for your external success.

In the next section, we will take a closer look at the role each PAEI subsystem plays within our human system.

The (P) role

You, as an individual, are a system, an "organization." And each organization has a purpose for which it exists. In a business organization the purpose is easier to identify because it can be measured by repetitive sales in a competitive market; if customers come back to buy your product—rather than choosing an alternative—this means you are satisfying a need. On a country level, the purpose of government (in a democracy) is to serve the needs of its citizens. This can be measured if the government is reelected. But in life, your personal purpose as a person is not always as easy to identify.

Each of us, within our own lives, serves multiple clients and entities: You, yourself, are your own client; your family, also a client, calls on you to do things for them; your employer and your country are also your clients. Often, our servitude gets confused. We serve one client more than the others, our career more than our immediate family. If this is planned, and done consciously, there is no problem. A problem begins when you are not happy with an outcome—when you feel side effects from how you chose to distribute time to your various clients, your different stakeholders, because each of them has a vested interest in what you do.

So we ask ourselves the question again: What am I here for, on this earth? And for whom?

There are many theories on this subject, which I will not analyze in this book. Rather, I will present what I believe. Your purpose is to serve beyond yourself. Do not ask yourself, "Why do I exist?" Ask, "For what do I exist?" For what is synonymous with why but focuses more effectively on who you really are, because you are what you do. You are the needs you satisfy. You are a father if you fulfill the functions of being a father. As a Serbian expression says, "A mother is not the one who gave birth but the one that raised the child."

Note that you need to serve yourself, too. "Im ein ani li, mi li," says one of the Jewish sages: "If I am not for myself, who is for me?" We need to serve the world but without forgetting our own needs in the process. We need to provide ourselves with a balanced life.

Regardless of the type of person you are, you must make the (P) vitamin work. You must perform the (P) role: putting into practice the purpose for which you exist. The purpose that makes you effective in the world. You must ask yourself: "What is the purpose of my life?" To answer this, you must question yourself further, "Who needs me? Who will cry if I die? Who will miss me?" Certain people will come to mind as you answer these questions. They are your "clients." They are the beings that you must focus on.

People are born twice: once physically and a second time when they realize why they were born, when they realize the purpose of their existence. The (P) vitamin inspires you to stop and ask yourself: "Why am I here on this earth? And for whom?" In both questions you are looking beyond yourself. You are looking to serve. When something serves itself only, it's like a cancer that takes energy only for its own purposes. "Vitamin (P)" prompts you to serve someone else's needs.

How can we verify that we are fulfilling our purpose in life? How do we discover our vocation in this area? Look for that which gives you energy. What is it that uplifts you and causes you to lose yourself while doing it? What service or activity makes you lose track of time, place, everything? Whatever it is, that is what you should do. That is you. That is what you exist for. And if you spend your life doing it, you will not feel that you have "worked and slaved" all your life. You will be self- actualized. You will feel satisfied.

When we act in the service of our purpose, we are able to enter a state of intense concentration—to the point of losing ourselves in the activity, where we lose track of time and space—while also experiencing great enjoyment and inner peace. We are integrated with our purpose. The stronger this integration, the closer we come to doing that for which we exist.

Another dimension of the (P) role is the ability to actually produce a desired result, thus making you effective in the short run. You get things done. You complete everything that is necessary in order to achieve gains in your life. Here, the (P) vitamin inspires you to stop talking and start doing, to make things happen in the physical world. This is the role that gets you moving. It's one thing to say, "I am going to go to the gym." That's good wishful thinking. The (P) vitamin will have you putting on your running shoes, or actually lifting the weights. It's about translating dreams into a reality. There is no progress without taking action and that's why the (P) role is an essential component of any coaching process. It is an essential subsystem within your coachee's system as a whole. Everything that contributes to getting things done now, and with a purpose, is (P): from bringing food to the table, to taking care of the kids, to taking the car to the mechanic, to cleaning the house, to making the evening meal.

The (P) style:

"I am a go-getter guy. I never let the foot off the gas pedal. Always creating and sustaining momentum. Can't really stand still for long, I am always in motion and crossing off things from my checklist." —Michael, 32 years old

Dominant in this personality is the person I like to call "the (P)roducer". This is the person who will say, "Let's go. Let's do it. Enough talking. Come on, guys. Let's get this done so we can move on." This type is task and now oriented. The (P) style can get very impatient if you want to stop and talk about the past or the future. He's moved by a continuous question in his head: "What do we need to do now?" These are the guys who shoot first and ask questions later. They are the doers, the achievers of the world.[1]

Main characteristics of (P)-oriented people:

- Goal/task/action oriented
- Value themselves by how much they do, not necessarily how well they do
- Achievers
- Industrious and productive
- Functional
- "Shoot first, and ask questions later" approach

Performing this role, to the exclusion of others, may cause the following side effects and result in what I call "the Lone Ranger:"[2]

---

1. For a deeper understanding of the PAEI roles and styles please see: Adizes, I.: *The Ideal Executive, Why You Cannot Be One and What to Do About It.* The Adizes Institute Publications, 2004 and Adizes, I.: *Management/ Mismanagement Styles: How to Identify a Style and What to Do About It.* Adizes Institute Publications, Santa Barbara, CA, 2004. Available from https://publications.adizes.com
2. Lone Ranger is a style people identify with in the USA because of the classic TV program. In Mexico, this style is known as "the one-man orchestra"; in Israel this style is known as "the bulldozer."

- Impatience
- Workaholism, constant motion
- Difficulty delegating
- Confusing quantity with quality
- Inability to stand still, to slow down, to pause, or to strategize

The (A) role

The (A) role is the second vitamin required for a healthy life. To be successful, you need structure, order. You need to put in place some good routines. Why? Imagine your life without systems and processes. Without them, you would quickly succumb to disorganization and chaos, and bring down those around you. It is the (A) vitamin that will have you saying things like: "I work out three times a week, on these days and at these times." or, "This is how much I earn; this is how much I spend every month, and this is how much I am saving." The (A) role allows you to be the (A)dministrator of your days, your workflow, your money, and your life.

Many people focus on earning more money or getting that desired salary raise, and then spend without establishing a budget (and become very inefficient along the way). This mindset is similar to companies that focus on increasing revenues without administering to their bottom line. They eventually find that they have been suffering losses without even knowing it. The role of (A) is to make sure you are efficient in the short term.

The (A) style:

> *"I have a good eye for detail and for finding what is out of place. A work not done perfect typically annoys me, as well as people who can't follow the rules and are always late."* —Ellen, 41 years old

Those folks with dominant (A) personalities are the linear thinkers. Every detail must be in place. They must be on time. Their life is regulated by laws and manuals (which, by the way, needn't be preexisting as they are continuously writing them in their own consciousness, in their minds). They attempt to systematize and organize everything in their lives.

Main characteristics of (A)-oriented people:

- Attention to detail
- Methodical and organized
- Follows the rules, principles, and guidelines
- Traditional and conservative
- Control oriented
- Prevention oriented, drawn to anticipating potential problems and pitfalls

If a person performs almost exclusively in this role, it may cause the following side effects (I call this style "the Bureaucrat"):

- Not seeing the forest for the trees: getting lost in the details, missing the big picture
- Rigidity
- Lack of creativity
- Only the tried and true seems valid
- Inflexible adherence to rules and regulations
- Slow decision-making

The (E) role

The first two vitamins, (P) and (A), contribute to effectiveness and efficiency, and allow you to take care of your needs and obligations in the short term. But what about your future? In a world of accelerated change, in which we are expected to deal with higher and higher rates of uncertainty, we need to stay flexible. We must be open to change. We must be open to reviewing our systems, our routines, and our way of doing things. These days it is not uncommon to build structures in our lives, only to discover that we need to adjust and fix them, or replace them altogether.

"A tree that is unbending is easily broken," says the Chinese proverb. And so, in these times of heightened change and uncertainty, we need to continuously and proactively adjust our lives, so that we can keep being effective in the future. This is where the (E) vitamin comes in. It provides flexibility, a fresh approach, an open mind, and a creative outlook.

The (E) style:

> *"Life is a miracle. I love how, at every turn, the magic—the new—can happen. It's a journey of learning where I get surprised time after time. I love playing with ideas and new possibilities. It excites me to continuously travel, seek for opportunities, and pursue new adventures"* —Matt, 33 years old

I like to call the person who is dominant in this role "the (E)ntrepreneur." They see the horizon. Voraciously creative, they are continuously excited by new ideas, but their feet may not be on the ground.

Main characteristics of (E)-oriented people:

- Visionaries, able to visualize new directions
- Proactive
- Big-picture thinkers
- Excited by adventure, change, and novelty
- Enthusiastic and stimulating
- Independent: need latitude, freedom of thought, and action
- Creative

- Often charismatic

If this role is exclusively performed it may cause the following side effects, and I call this style "the arsonist":

- Poor follow-up on projects, weak implementation
- Cycles through periods of enthusiasm, followed by periods of disillusionment
- Keeps a chaotic schedule, impulsively violates any agenda (even his own)
- Inhibits progress when their "why not" attitude takes over, impulsivity may cause them to chase too many exciting ideas and opportunities at once

The (I) role

As change increases in the external world, we become busier and more absorbed by it. Our job alone can take most and sometimes all of our vital energy. The rate of change may cause us to feel tense, like we are being sucked into a rat race, and leave us utterly exhausted. Thus, putting energy into the outside can cause us to fall apart on the inside. And that's where the (I), the fourth essential vitamin of PAEI, comes into the picture.

We must integrate ourselves on the inside before we can integrate ourselves with the outside. If we try only to change the outside, we will create a "space syndrome" within ourselves: expanding our outer margins but collapsing at our core. We see this in individuals who don't invest in personal growth, who seek progress almost exclusively in their careers: they grow, grow, grow, very fast, and then all of a sudden: BOOM! Divorce, nervous exhaustion, unhappiness, stressed to the core. As one of my very successful entrepreneurial clients lamented to me: "All I remember about my children is when they were born and when they got married. In between I have no memories."

> *"I sought coaching after recovering from severe burnout and my wife of twenty years giving me an ultimatum. I used to work nonstop and was literally falling apart. I learned self-care the hard way."* —John, 49 years old

As I mentioned in the intro to this chapter, energy is fixed at any point in time. Even the most energetic person has only twenty-four hours in a day.

If you are falling apart inside, this state of being takes all your energy and you cannot deal with the outside. Imagine having a conflict with your spouse over breakfast. How much energy do you have when you get to work? Consider the energy it takes to deal with a bad cold: sneezing, coughing, feeling miserable. How much energy do you have left to make strategic plans for your career?

To begin to make order out of these inevitable imbalances, the (I) role focuses on what you need to be a whole being. The (I) takes a reading of both your external conditions (work, relationships, financial obligations) and your internal conditions (mindset, psychological state, health), and analyzes how your energy is being allocated.

The (I) role is the vitamin that can lead you to integration. And what is absolute integration, if not love?

When we experience love there are no boundaries between us and the object of our love. A mother can suddenly feel the need to call her son in another town. How does she know that he is having a problem? She feels it within her love for him.

Love, which is associated with the heart both figuratively and literally, is the manifestation of absolute integration. I do not know why the shape of a heart is the symbol for love, but it is. What I do know is that in order to focus on the heart you need to stop focusing on the brain. The more you think and reason, the less you can feel love.

Love is experienced in the silence of the moment. Stop thinking and start feeling.

Look at a baby. When a person whom the baby does not recognize approaches it, the baby focuses hard on that person and feels him or her. No thinking is involved. No reasoning of the cost value of the relationship. The baby just feels and if it does not feel love, it starts crying.

Feel more. Think less. That is the route to (I). That is the route to (I)ntegration.

There are many courses that teach how to listen, how to communicate. They are good, and can be helpful, but they are processed with the brain. True (I) is spiritual. It is the expression of love. No thinking. No judging. Just loving.

And how do you know if you are loving versus just acting in a loving way?

The expression, in western languages I know, is that "life is give and take." Why do you take your kids to the circus? So you can write it in your diary? "On such and such a date I took them to the circus, so now they owe me." Do you take them so that when you get old they will feel the need to take care of you? God forbid, right? In the Sephardic language there is an expression which my mother used to say, "Dios piadoso, solo no esperar de las creaturas" (Merciful God, only not to expect from the children).

It is expectations that ruin love.

You took your children to the circus to give them joy. Their happiness is what makes you feel happy too. That is your reward. In a loving relationship in the giving is the taking. It is simultaneous. That is why a Buddhist might say to you: "Thank you for allowing me to serve you." Through serving you, he received a rewarding experience.

In love you give and expect nothing back. Your reward is in the loving.

There is a difference between loving and liking.

You like because of.

You love in spite of.

So, who is this "me" that is beyond what I do, no matter how well I serve the world?

You are your spirit. The body is just the "box" that carries your spirit. When you focus on your spirit you realize you are just a piece and a part of something more, something bigger than yourself. That you belong to something beyond you that is absolute. You are being driven by this absolute force.

What was there before the Big Bang, when the universe was created?

Time and space started with the Big Bang, which means that before the Big Bang nothing was bounded by space or time. This unbounded "space" was infinite. And what is not bound by time and space is LOVE.

Love creates everything …

Look at an artist in any field. What compels the artist to paint? Or write music? Love. Prohibit the artist from practicing their art and see how they feel.

And what about an entrepreneur? He (or she) starts a company. What drove him or her to do so? Was it money? The company is probably losing money and the whole enterprise is probably more likely than not to fail. So what was it? Love of an idea. LOVE.

Love creates. Hate destroys.

I believe our sole purpose in life is to love and to be loved. Show a criminal love and see him or her melt. There are programs in some prisons in which the prisoners are each allowed to raise a dog. This program has shown reduced incidents of prison riots. There are stories of prisoners who have fallen in love with the birds that visit their window.

When deprived of love we cannot grow. Babies deprived of love are underdeveloped. Criminals are people who were deprived of love and fell apart. They disintegrated: socially, economically, and/or emotionally.

The solution is not punishment to bring on more disintegration, but rather, mental and socioeconomic integration.

Love and hate are not opposites. Hate is the absence of love the way darkness is the absence of light. Do not hate hate. Just love and hate will disappear.

How much or how "far" you love (i.e., how much or how far along you are in your integration), is a function of your consciousness. Some people love only money. Others go one step further and love their family. Still others also love their community. And some go beyond all of this and also love their country—and are willing to sacrifice their life for this love. And some expand their consciousness to include love for birds, and mountains, and fish, and flowers, air, and water.

How conscious are you? How much love do you have to give?

There is no internal integration without meta-awareness: your ability to observe yourself and your mental and emotional processes so you can make peace with them. Observe your subsystems.

If you work ten hours on what is outside of you, then work one hour on what is inside of you—so the inside doesn't fall apart. You get your "act together" when you align and integrate your internal world. You become much stronger, and when you integrate internally you free your energy to help you deal with the outside.

In the Adizes Methodology, the (I) role helps you regulate these two dimensions, the outside and the inside. Meditation is an important component of this role. If you think meditation is a waste of time, think again. Think of it as an investment with a big ROI. In fact, meditation is as important as sleeping. It repairs you; it integrates you, and it makes you stronger. If you incorporate meditation into your routine, you'll make fewer mistakes. You'll find that you are no longer crawling through the day in pieces. The team that wins is the one that has it all together. The same goes for you, you will win when you are integrated—when you have it all together.

Just like the other roles, the (I) role needs to be worked on and developed. Some people are born with a more developed (I) role, but for the rest of us this is not the case. But it's worth the effort. Cultivating this internal integration improves your long-term efficiency in life. The less disintegration there is within your thinking, emotional, and body processes, the better equipped you will be to relate to others. You will be less[3] distracted by inner turmoil, and have more energy to tackle the challenges of life.

Let's look at this in terms of a company, a big corporation. What is a company's biggest asset? It's not its technology, nor its money, nor its brand. A company's biggest asset is its people. Its culture. In the same way, your biggest asset is not your money, nor your education. It's your mindset. Are you internally integrated? Are you together? How strong is your own self-leadership?

---

3. We say "less" on purpose because we are human beings, not machines. We can never reach zero inner turmoil. Welcome to life. But with Adizes self-coaching, our inner turmoil can be managed and converted into a learning experience, making us stronger as we learn from our mistakes.

How does the (I) role help to create self-leadership?

In our internal, intrapersonal realm, the (I) role creates self-trust and self-respect by:

- Developing our awareness of our strengths and weaknesses.
- Showing us our unique talents and gifts—as well as our limitations.
- Managing our mental models, our beliefs, our values, and how we perceive and interpret our reality.
- Harnessing our internal conflicts (which are inevitable) and preventing us from allowing our mistakes to become destructive, converting them instead into constructive learning experiences.
- Encouraging us to slow down and relax in difficult situations.

In our external, interpersonal realm, the (I)ntegrator creates mutual trust and mutual respect by:

- Facilitate how we relate to others—not only with our minds, but also with our hearts.
- Catalyzing collaboration, helping us work within a team, not just as an individual.
- Encouraging listening, empathy, and support.
- Harnessing inevitable conflicts with other people in a constructive way.

The (I) style:

> *"I am passionate about understanding myself and others, finding out what makes us humans tick, and how we can make relationships better. I always had a helping orientation and found myself naturally in Human Resources Development roles, injecting as much heart and a collaborative spirit as possible into the teams I work with."* —Jeanna, 39 years old

The (I) role can be passive and/or active. Passive means the person works well with others, is conscious and sensitive, and willing to understand another person's point of view. An active (I) is a person who can integrate others, who can bring people together and build a team.

I call the person with a dominant (I) personality "the Integrator." The main characteristics of (I)-oriented people are:

- Awareness of interpersonal dynamics
- Ability to be reasonable and supportive
- Patient, with good listening skills
- Empathetic
- Skilled in harmonizing dissent
- Proactive
- Prone to foster collaboration and teamwork, a "togetherness" spirit

When the (I) role is the sole, dominant style the side effects listed below may occur. I call this "the Super Follower," one who does not lead but rather follows the crowd.[4] "Super Followers" tend to be:

- Laser focused on the human side of things (to the detriment of other aspects of their life and business).
- Conflict avoiders who pursue agreement (or the illusion of) sometimes at all costs.
- Accommodating, noncommittal.
- Hypersensitive to rejection.
- People pleasers, putting people and feelings above tasks (even when this is inappropriate).

---

4. In Mexico this person is called "pez enjabonado." A soapy, slippery fish which is difficult to catch.

THE INCOMPATIBILITY OF THE FOUR PAEI ROLES

Each of the four PAEI roles is necessary in a person's life, and the four together are the recipe for good self-management. By necessary, I mean that if any one role is not performed (or is underperformed), a pattern of self-mismanagement will begin to unfold.

Why is it so hard to have your life "together"? To have these four roles synchronized, and to achieve success in life? Why is no one perfect?

The four roles, by their very natures, are incompatible in the short run and thus mutually inhibitive. In other words, the ability to excel at one of the PAEI roles often impedes one's ability to excel in one or more of the others.

(P) and (I) incompatibility

For example, the (P) role and the (I) role are incompatible. Have you ever attended a personal-development seminar? You spend three days being taught how to be a better (I): how to relate better to your loved ones and be a more compassionate human being. Then back to real life. One day you are at home, working late, focused on an imminent deadline, and what happens? Interruptions. Your family needs you. You become short and easily irritated with your spouse or children. You cannot be understanding or accommodating because your deadline is looming. Under this time pressure to (P)erform and generate results, you become harsh and (I)ntegration is given a lower priority. In this situation, the (P) is squeezing out the (I).

Notice that people do not often fall in love while under pressure, while running to catch a bus or a plane. They fall in love on vacation, while walking the beach at sunset.

Notice, also, that people in large cities often feel lonely despite having millions of people all around them. Look at the bumper stickers on the cars in those cities. Over and over you will see the word, LOVE.

Love Jesus. Or love whatever. As well, the bigger the city the more dogs per capita. People need love. They need someone to wiggle their tail and show happiness when they arrive home at night.

But why does this happen? In large cities, the (P) role dominates. There is a lot of pressure to catch that bus, to find that parking spot, to work and perform. Because of the constant pressure to rush, (I) is given a lower priority. Once again, the (P) squeezes out the (I).

Do you want to find the love of your life? Go where there is peace. Go to a museum. Go to an art gallery. Take an art class. Take a vacation. Don't go to a bar. Too much noise. Too much pressure. It might happen. It does happen. But that is more luck than success.

(P) and (E) incompatibility

The (P) and the (E) roles are also incompatible. How many times have you said, "I'm working so hard, I have no time for fun or to learn something new?" Maybe you would like to learn an instrument, or study a new language, or try a salsa class—but you are so busy that you never find the time. This is a sign that your (P) is at brutal levels and that you have no time for anything else.

The reverse is also true. The (E) role can threaten the (P) role. (E), with its never-ending capacity to make new plans and come up with new ideas, often sets too many things in motion simultaneously, and (P) can't get anything done. Nothing is ever finished. (E) can put too many balls in the air (and then you end up with them all on the floor).

(P) and (A) incompatibility

And what about the (P) and the (A) roles? Are they also incompatible? When there is a crisis, you have to act, (P), you must be effective. Being organized and systematic (A) is a luxury you don't have in an emergency. If you see a person getting electrocuted in the kitchen you just grab a wooden stick or broom as fast as you can and, BAM! You separate them from the electrical source without touching them. You have to act quickly. You have to use your (P) skills. There is no time to google a solution or look for a step-by-step procedure! In an emergency, (P) must act. But what about (A)? Under what circumstances does the (A) role undermine (P)? These are the cases where the (A) is over-emphasized and you spend more time on forms and papers than actually doing the job.

(A) and (E) incompatibility

Next, we come to the (A) and the (E) roles incompatibility. Innovation and change require minimal limitations. The more rules, policies, and routines there are, the less flexible and able one is to deviate from those requirements and explore new terrains.

> *"My husband is a very structured guy. He created a routine for himself—for the weekdays and the weekends—that he's been keeping for years. He is a control freak that likes to have every hour programmed. You can't mess with his schedule. Problem is, he is rigid. And as a professional graphic designer and website builder, his whole profession is in turmoil, and he is gradually being replaced by sites who offer user-friendly, ready-to-use websites. Nobody calls him for a logo anymore, as you can buy them ready-made on hundreds of sites. He is becoming obsolete but because of his rigidity he is unable to change his weekly structures to start investing time in reconverting his profession."* —Melissa, 39 years old

The above example illustrates how, as you lock yourself in (A), your ability to be proactive and effective in the long run becomes limited. Ritualized behaviors inhibit change. Thus, (A) endangers (E), and (E) endangers (A): routine cannot develop because what we do and how we do it is always changing.

(A) and (I) incompatibility

Now let's take look at the incompatibility of (A) and (I). If you want organic integration as a family, for example, you need to sit down and talk through any issues that come up with your family members. The more you do this, the less you will need to rely on rules. And conversely, the more you use rules and compliance to guide your children's behavior, the less open communication you can expect to have around the table (and therefore the less opportunities to integrate as a family).

Another way of looking at (I) and (A) incompatibility: both produce efficiency, but (A) is mechanistic. (A) achieves efficiency by organizing things, through following the rules and sticking to procedures. In contrast, (I) is organic. (I) achieves efficiency through love and care, not through enforced policies or standard-operating procedures. Religion starts as an (I) system, but over time it gets systematized into rules and rituals, which are governed by (A). And then what happens? People follow the rituals but forget about or ignore the spirituality. Corrupt religious leaders who work the system are an example of (A) squeezing out (I).

PAEI AS A CODE FOR PERSONALITY STYLE

As a result of these incompatibility issues, most people are naturally good at or comfortable with one or two roles and tend to exhibit heavily those roles in their behavior. It is these dominant roles that characterize a person's "style." Which roles they excel in is driven by the dominant glands they are born with. Dr. Elliot Abravanel, MD,[5] attributes the (P) style to the adrenalin gland, the (A) style to the pituitary gland, the (E) style to the thyroid gland, and the (I) style to the gonadal gland. In other words, we are born with certain

---

5. Abravanel, E. Dr. Abravanel's: *Body Type Diet and Lifetime Nutrition Plan*, 1983 Revised Edition, New York, NY: Bantam

predispositions to certain styles. We won't change easily and completely and become someone else. We can improve our style and become more well-rounded, less-extreme, performing only one role. That is what people call "change", but for a total change of one's personality—for an (E) personality to become an (I) personality, for instance—we must be reborn.

In the Adizes Methodology, a "personality code" is built out of your four roles by measuring how many of your traits fall into each role. This measurement is rated on a scale of 0 to 9 (0 being least dominant, 9 being most dominant), producing a combined PAEI personality code for each person. If I am a great in the (P) and (A) roles, measured at levels 8 and 7 respectively, but I am completely unable to perform (E) or (I) roles (both are at 0), then my PAEI code will be: 8700, or PA00 (P-8, A-7, E-0, I-0).

The Adizes coding system denotes roles we excel in with capital letters, roles we meet the threshold in with lowercase letters, and roles we are unable to perform at all with a zero. So as shown in the example above, the code is PA00. (If the result had been 2 and 3 for (E) and (I), respectively, then the code would have been 8723, or PAei.)

While one person may excel in foreseeing the future (paEi), another may excel at organizing (pAei), and still a third may excel at harmonizing relationships (paeI), and so on. One person, in other words, can be predominantly a (P)roducer, an (A)dministrator, an (E)ntrepreneur, or an (I)ntegrator—or any combination of these roles—but he CANNOT be a (PAEI) all by himself. No one is perfect. We all have our strengths and weaknesses.[6]

Unfortunately, for any given person, a role can be completely missing, totally squeezed out, threatened into extinction, or never fully

---

6. To find your particular style, take the ALIS tests at the Adizes Institute website, https://adizes.com

developed. Furthermore, change fuels our internal conflict: the more hustle and bustle in our lives, the less the four roles are in balance.

Thus, the difference between people who successfully manage their lives—people who are truly self-leaders—and people who mismanage their lives is one of degree and circumstance. A person with no zeros in their code—that is, a person who is capable of performing all four roles even if they excel in only one of them—is potentially a functional person without being perfect, as long as their PAEI personality code conforms to their job or life demands.

To be a surgeon, for instance, requires one to be decisive and move forward until the end of a task. It requires a strong (P). The same goes for a fighter jet pilot. A psychotherapist, on the other hand, has to feel the patient's feelings and constantly maneuver how he or she administers the therapy. Thus, an (EI) personality is needed, because the therapist needs to be willing to establish the therapeutic process over the long run. Imagine a person with a (P) personality trying to do psychotherapy. Or a person with an (EI) personality doing heart surgery ...

When coaching people, the personality style of the coachee initially has to be assumed. Once it has been established, the coach should preferably have a personality that *complements* the personality of the coachee.[7] When this is the case, the coach will be able to identify the weaknesses of the coachee much easier.

In the Adizes Methodology, self-management means to work on oneself, to improve oneself. If you excel in one or more roles, you should

---

7. Provided that the coach, of course, has a healthy PAEI code of its own, with no blanks. Ideally, a big (I). In this way, generally speaking, the coach can flexibly communicate with all types of coachees—although they may be particularly suited to help those whose style is complementary to them. Coaches, according to their PAEI code, can specialize in different styles of coaching: PaeI make great coaches who help their coachees produce action and results; pAeI are best suited to help coachees create structure and get organized; paEI coaches are best at helping coachees connect to their mission and unlock their possibilities and options.

also be able to meet at least the threshold requirements of the other roles. Why? In addition to the possibility that life may call upon you to perform one of your weaker roles in an emergency, you must also be able to relate to those who naturally excel in the roles that are harder for you.

As a result of your innate gifts and your genetic predisposition, you will most likely have a particular orientation toward one or two of the PAEI roles, but you should not be lacking in any of them if you want a healthy life.

Let me illustrate this with an example. This book was written in the midst of the 2020 COVID-19 pandemic. Imagine this crisis caught you with a blank in your (A) role. Imagine (A) was never your strong point, that you are pretty bad in this area, and that you never invested in developing it even a little bit. You let it slide. Now, faced with the Covid turmoil, if you had developed the (A) side of your personality even minimally, you might have thought to sit down and create a simple budget and forecast your cash flow for the months ahead. Now, in the midst of the pandemic, you lose your job—perhaps the entire industry that you work in is shut down—and you are suddenly forced to reorganize your finances. In such a situation, with survival at stake and without at least the minimum amount of (A) skills, you would be woefully unprepared. Bad enough if you are single but what if you have a family that is relying on you?[8] Such is the importance of self-management, of proactivity, and of becoming a well-rounded person.

---

8. If you are married or planning to be in a relationship, having zeros in your PAEI code can be bad news for you. Predictable troubles lie ahead. I recommend that you read *The Power of Opposites*, to learn how the Adizes methodology can help you build a healthy relationship, based on the specific combination of both your style and your partner's.

THE PERFECT PERSON DOES NOT AND CANNOT EXIST (BUT THAT DOES NOT PROHIBIT YOU FROM WORKING ON YOURSELF!)

"Everybody is ignorant, only on different subjects." —Will Rogers

Because of incompatibility and conflict between the PAEI roles, the perfect person does not and cannot exist. Not even the most advanced gurus or self-actualized people in the world can excel in all four roles and be "Full PAEI" AT THE SAME TIME; but as a rule, those who are naturally drawn to leading, typically excel in (I) plus one or two other roles. You can be a statesman who integrates people around a central vision (paEI), or a little-league coach who inspires young athletes (PaeI), or a well-loved administrator who keeps the ship afloat (pAeI). We are all leaders if we have (I), and we apply our (I) style to situations that call for it in our own unique way.

How does an individual become integrated?[9] By becoming "together" inside. By becoming whole inside. When internal integration of your mind, body and heart is achieved, then there is good "teamwork" going on inside of you. You know who you are, what your gifts are, and what your limitations are. And you learn and grow continuously. Self-management and self-leadership point to higher and higher levels of internal (I)ntegration. When you are listening to someone your body is present, your mind is present, and your heart is present. All of these intelligences are integrated and working together—with you as the director of the orchestra. You develop the wisdom to know which energy or role should be flexibly used in any given situation. You can successfully perform all four roles—some at a level of excellence,

---

9. In a corporation, the answer is to work with others who complement your PAEI code: an integrated and complementary team. No individual can be "Full PAEI," but two individuals can pool their strengths (if they have no blanks) and together create "Full PAEI." Similarly, in a marriage, the answer is to find a partner who complements you (as long as neither has blanks in their code) so that, between the two of you, a good PAEI mix may be reached.

others just at the threshold level—and you have the wisdom to harmonize between all of these dynamics.

What is the purpose of coaching, and of personal development work? To become perfect? No. To become whole? Yes. In terms of PAEI, becoming whole means following a process: "First, I find out what my strengths are. Second, I discover what my weaknesses are. Then, I work on becoming well-rounded (again, not to become "perfect," but to become "whole") by capitalizing on my strengths, and by building my weaker areas up to at least a threshold—so if I am called on to perform them, situationally, I can do so." And why is this so? "Because working on my weaknesses has its limitations. I may not be able to develop them to the level of excellence; but I can certainly develop them to the level of functionality. I can meet the minimum necessary standards so I can live and work with others." To truly be whole what you really need is a complementary team. You must always be aiming to surround yourself with people who complement you. A mistake many people make is to try to develop their weaknesses with the goal of becoming self-sufficient. They may achieve their desired self-sufficiency, but they will not bring a weak area to a point of excellence and complete success. They will more likely reach a level of "good/average." This is why surrounding oneself with others who compliment your style is always a beneficial solution.

Let's say you are a very strong (PaEi) person, but your (A) and (I) roles are practically below threshold. Your coaching goal, then, should be to improve yourself in those areas. Otherwise, it won't be long before life shocks you in some way through these two roles. Your bank calls to tell you they are closing your credit limit because you are not settling your debts in time (due to your low (A) role). Your spouse surprises you with a request for a divorce (due to your inability to use your (I) role). It's in your best interest to work on these weak areas and build them up to at least the minimum. If you want to excel you need to complement yourself—thus the importance of marriage and building a complementary team with your partner.

If you are below threshold in any of the four roles, then the best course of action would be to consult a psychologist or a psychiatrist, as your needs are more complex and are beyond the scope of this book.

But can people really improve? No one can change entirely. We cannot convert a big (P) into a big (I), but we can improve the weaker roles. As it is true that things can get worse, it is also true that they can get better. Remember, we are not talking about converting a "mow you down/locomotive" (PE) into an "infinitely patient/empathetic" (AI). He won't become that. But just as he is at risk of going "off the rails," he is equally capable of becoming "more together."

Some folks change only when faced with the high cost of not changing. It happens when they are cornered by life—backed up against a wall. Some people need to have a small heart attack before they can convince themselves to begin the process of quitting smoking. Or a spouse handing them the divorce papers. Some people need a strong wake-up call. When one has not wanted to or been able to change proactively (which in this case means the developing of one's weaker PAEI roles), change can often be triggered through one of life's little ultimatums. It's better not to wait for the heart attack before you quit smoking. It's better to be proactive, rather than reactive. Most people know how to get out of a hole. A proactive person knows how not to fall into the hole in the first place.

But still, all of the above is easier said than done, right? What's more common in the average human being? Internal disharmony. Inner conflict. And this inner turmoil tends to become self-sabotaging and self-destructive. Our heart, for instance, may be pushing us to spend more time with our family (I), but our mind is visualizing the future it wants (E), and making calculations to achieve this future (A) (which will require more money), and our (P) role may be hijacked by any of the other three roles. Or the opposite may happen if the (P) role is on autopilot, directionless, impulsively acting for the sake of action, without "listening" to what the other roles are saying. In such a situation, a family might be neglected (I), and a dream might never be fulfilled (E), or the bills might not get paid (A).

Can you begin to see how decision-making is suboptimal when you are not internally integrated? Do these examples properly illustrate how dangerous it can be to mismanage your life, and make decisions in a chaotic fashion? This brings us to our next chapter, in which we will explore the need for a systemic decision-making tool.

HOW WE MAKE DECISIONS: THE FOUR VOICES IN OUR HEAD

A lot has been written in psychological and spiritual literature about the topic of identity, and how we tend to get confused listening to "the voices in our head."[10] I suggest that there are four PAEI voices in our head: one that tells us what to do, another that tells us how to do it, a third that tells us by when to have it done, and the last that wonders who is the right person to do it.

Imagine you need to make a decision, listen to what's going on between your ears:

- Voice #1, (P): "I don't know, **what** should I do about this?"
- Voice #2, (A): "And **how** the heck am I going to do this?"
- Voice #3, (E): "And also, **when** should I do this?"
- Voice #4, (I): "**Who** will give me trouble if I do this? What will people say, or think?"

10. See, for instance, Michael Singer's The Untethered Soul: the journey beyond yourself, Oakland: CA: New Harbinger, 2007

So there is not just one "guy" in there, there are actually four! No wonder so many people live in a constant state of tension and anxiety, where making any type of decision becomes a mess.

The problem is that if you are unaware of this PAEI mechanism, it's easy for you to let these voices go on fighting with each other, and stay in conflict in your head. The next thing you know, you can't sleep, because the four voices are still going at it and putting you in the middle. So what is the solution? You can't single out just one of the voices, and you will never have peace if you try to ignore them.

What does it mean, then, to be healthy? Can the four voices ever "sing" in harmony? Keep in mind, they will never sing the same note. They will always sing different notes, but they can sing together in harmony. They can sing notes that complement each other …

If you look at your hand, what do you see? Look at your hand, palm up, with your fingers straight and touching each other. Go to a church of any denomination and look at the paintings or the sculptures of saints. They are holding a hand in front of them with the fingers together. What are they telling you? Be different, but together. That is their blessing.

Each finger is different, but to use our hand properly we need to accept our four different fingers and allow them to work together. Each finger (i.e., each PAEI role) does something the other fingers cannot do as well. There is synergy when they work together. In the Middle East the stretched hand with fingers together is called a hamsa. Women often wear this open-palm symbol as an amulet. It can also be found on the entrance to a home. It is a blessing: Be different, but together.

In the Middle East, when they curse someone, they spread their fingers and put their hand in front of the face they are cursing as if to say: be different and not together.

The difference between a blessing and a curse is only two inches: Are we "different, but together" or "different and not together"?

It is not fusion that we want, but integration: for each of us to maintain our identity, but cooperate. By integrating the gifts that each role can bring the best decision can be made—a better decision than any one of the roles could have made alone.

There are religions, political ideologies, that promote togetherness but not diversity: We can be together only if we are all the same. This is fascism, racism, and fanatic religion. Sameness.

Without diversity there is no growth. No cross-pollination. Look at a desert. Sameness. What grows there? Look at a jungle. You see the difference?

In order for a decision to be implemented to its highest potential, the decision needs to be well-rounded. A well-rounded decision is one that is taken from an integrated PAEI viewpoint—hearing all four voices in coordination, singing in harmony—and therefore answers all the questions that are imperative to ask.

The imperatives are: what, how, who, and by when.[11]

Leaving one or more of these imperatives out produces an incomplete, defective decisioin that most probably will not produce the desired outcome. Take leaving out the by when imperative. Your (E) voice will push you in the direction of wanting things done yesterday; type (E) usually gets upset when something has not been done yet, whatever it is. The (P) voice wants it now. The (A) voice, preoccupied with the details, believes it will take at least a year to get that very same thing done. (A) will push you to put the decision on hold until you collect more information.

---

11. The fifth imperative, why, impacts them all.

Since the by when imperative has not been finalized, each voice retains its own expectation of when the task should be accomplished, which can be a source of inner conflict and indecision.

THE SEQUENCE OF DECISION-MAKING AND THE FIVE IMPERATIVES

What did I mean when I said you must "hear all four voices in coordination"? I meant that to make a well-rounded decision we need to address each of the decision-making imperatives, and we must do so in a certain sequence.

First, we must define what it is that we are trying to resolve. Without a clear definition of what we are trying to do, we cannot determine why we are trying to do it.

Systematic Decision-Making Process
The sequence of "WHAT, HOW, BY WHEN" and "WHO" should be prioritized first.

	E	P	I	E	A
START >	WHY	WHAT*	HOW	BY WHEN	WHO

◯ Tentative decision   ◯ Aligned decision   ◯ Finalized decision

"Why what?" is a familiar response to the question "Why?". Think about this for a moment: "Why what?" What is the answer? First we must determine what we are concerned with. Then, we can determine why we are concerned with it.

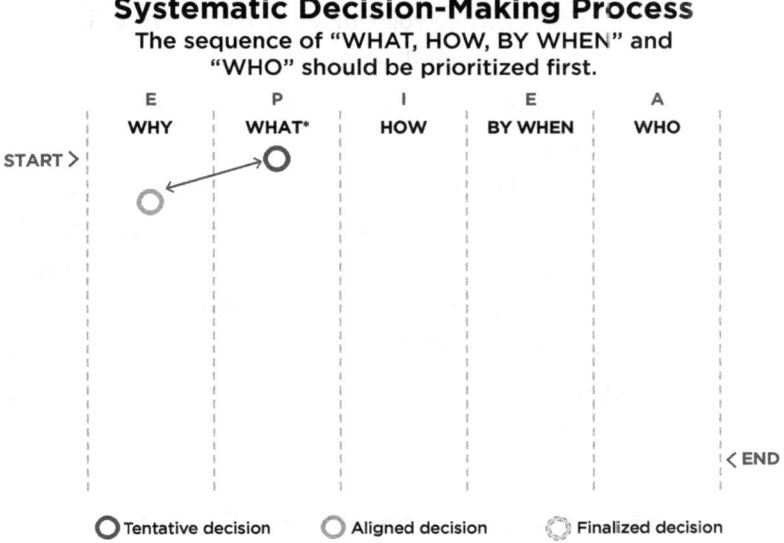

Based on the answers we get from asking *why*, we may go back and redefine our *what* imperative.

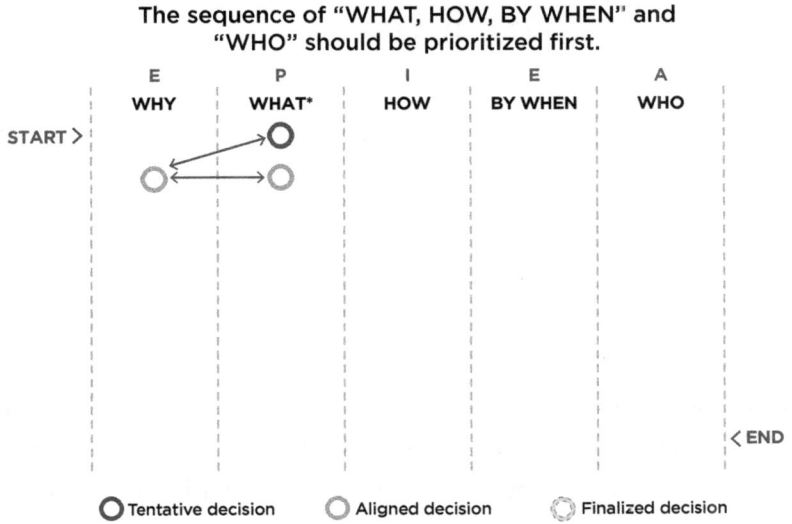

Now that we know what we are going to do and why we are going to do it, we must determine which imperative to address next. The sequence differs from case to case.

Imagine that you need someone you can really trust to install a security system in your home. If you don't know of a reputable company, the next imperative in your decision-making process is the who? To answer the who, you need to choose an installation company and contact them. Now, once you choose a company to contact to discuss the possibility of this installation, you may need to review and change the what, they may need to order parts before they can do the installation). Furthermore, the installer's PAEI personality will most likely impact how the installation will be done, and by when, which, de facto, will impact what exactly will be done. It might even alter the why (Why is this installation being done at all?)

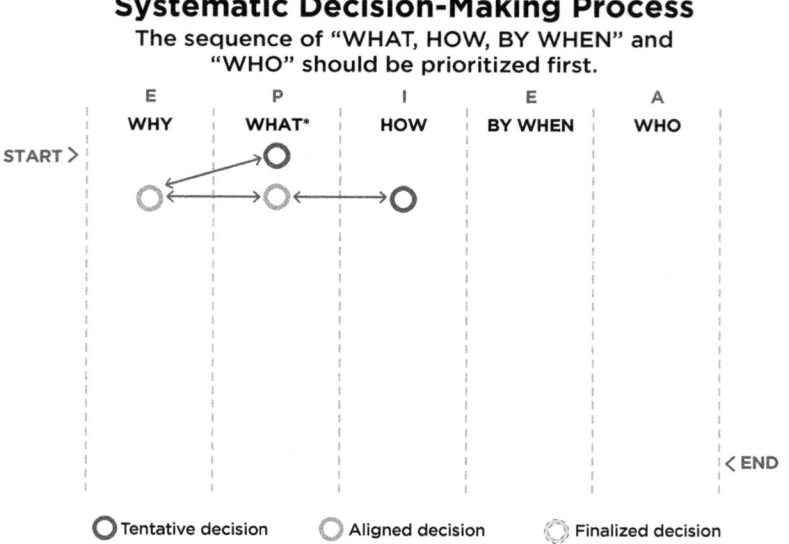

Consider another example: You have a crisis in your personal life that must be dealt with as soon as possible. In the case of an emergency, one of the most important imperatives to be dealt with is the by when imperative.

In each decision-making case, we must decide which of the imperatives is the most important to address first, next, thereafter, and so on: this is the sequence.

A decision is complete, finalized, and made in a healthy, integrated way when we have satisfied all of the imperatives: what is that we need to do, why we need to do it, who will be responsible for doing it, by when must it be done, and how it will be done.

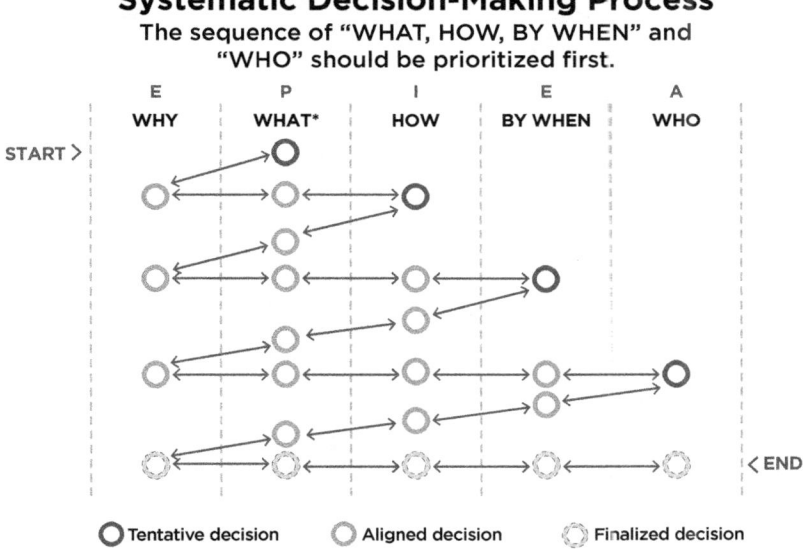

Notice that the decision-making process is not linear. It goes back and forth. As Vladimir Ilyich Lenin, the leader of the Soviet Revolution, said: "It is necessary sometimes to take one step backward to take two steps forward."

Foundational Tool #3:

The 8 Step Decision-Making Process

To make a decision you need to follow a process, and it doesn't matter if we are talking about a big decision or a small one. Whether you are choosing your living room furniture, or making your continuing education plans, or deciding where you are going to live, this eight-step process will help you to make the most effective decision.

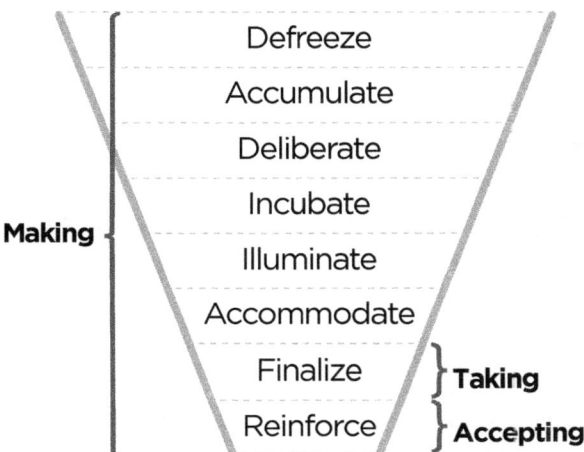

The process of decision-making is like a funnel. At the beginning there is a lot of uncertainty and we really don't have an idea what to do. Through the process from *defreeze* to *reinforce* we reduce the uncertainty, one step at a time, until the decision is finalized and reinforced. There is still some uncertainty left, but not as much as it was when we began the process.

Interestingly, in the English language we say "decision-making." In Spanish and French it is "decision-taking," and in Hebrew it is "decision-accepting." Who is right? All. But they refer to different parts of the process and thus they are all useful.

First step – Defreeze

I have created the word defreeze. It's a word that doesn't exist in the dictionary. I am not using unfreeze because Kurt Levin already used it for something else.

We each have a left side to our brain and a right side to our brain.[12] We create (E) and feel (I) with the right side of our brain. We act (P) and logically process information (A) with the left side of our brain. We spend most of our time on the left side of our brain. When we need to make a decision (which is a creative process, (E)), we need to stop the action, (P), and the activity that is happening on the left side of our brain (PA) and move to the right side (EI). This is because when we are making a decision, and thinking in terms of options and problem-solving, we need the creativity of our right-side brain. This doesn't happen automatically: It's like a train changing tracks; you have to consciously and intentionally slow down the left side—slow down the action—and move to the right side. That's what defreezing is, the slowing down of the action and logical linear-thinking.

---

12. This is at best an approximation of how the brain functions. It's simplified here to make the point.

Intuitively, you already know this. Anytime you have to make a major decision, you probably go home, shut the door, mute the smartphone, and take a deep breath. Some people take off their shoes and pour a drink.

This makes you ready. Ready for what? To start accumulating information, which is the next step.

Most of our creative thinking is done when driving home. Or taking a shower, or in meditation. Common denominator: we are relaxed and free from interruptions and interferences. Not strange that Archimedes had his eureka moment in a bath tub.

Those that can't find a quiet time, safe from interruptions during the day will have insomnia during the night. They fall asleep but wake up in the middle of the night and start thinking. What happened? When they fell asleep they were defreezing. And now they are awake and start creatively thinking what, why, how, etc to do.

Second step – Accumulate

Now you begin putting all our options on the table. You accumulate information. You ask yourself: "What do I want here?" Imagine you are an educator who delivers presentations with computers. You want to buy a new computer. Which option do you like best? You look at all of the available models that may be relevant for you and end up with a list of ten options.

Third step – Deliberate

Once you have accumulated, you can start deliberating the information. You take all the information you have accumulated and try to narrow it down. So you have ten different computers, and now you put them into two different categories: desktop or laptop. Which style of computer do you really want? You try to narrow it down because a mind can only handle so much information at any point in time.

When you have too much information you cannot make a decision. Ten models are too many, so you must make the information more manageable. You simplify your decision by assigning each of the ten models to one of the two categories.

You could also segment your options by criteria. What are the things you are looking for in your ideal computer? These could be: size and portability, looks stylish, speed, screen resolution, battery life, storage size, price.

You could then go further and classify the above by "must haves" versus "nice to haves," in terms of specifications.

Because you travel a lot and like cool gear, it's a must for you that the computer is very portable. You want to look professional, so you need a computer that looks good at your trainings. It also needs to be fast and have a good battery life, so you can work unplugged on the road. And regarding disk size, you don't need much, because you store everything in the cloud, so "storage size" is only a "nice to have" for you. In this step you make patterns. In the accumulate phase you accumulate all what at the time you thought was relevant information needed for making the decision. In deliberate you put the information in patterns. That is how you narrow down the information you need to consider.

One way to have patterns is by PAEI. The P pattern is what happened, if the decision you are making is to diagnose the problem. Then the pattern how it happened, when it happened , with whom it happened.

There could be any other way to pattern the ingredients of the decision depending on what is the decision you are making. Just look at the data you accumulated. It should stand out.

Fourth step – Incubate

This is where you say, "I cannot think about this anymore. I have to sleep on it." It's a sort of "catching your breath." You have exhausted yourself; you have used up all your energy, and now you have to sleep on it. In Spanish they say: Tengo que consultar con la almohada ("I have to consult my pillow."). When you cannot make an immediate decision about a plan or an idea, you sleep on it. You need to step back from it a little bit. Take a little distance from it. You've been too close to it for too long.

Fifth step – Illuminate

Then comes the stage that psychologists call the "Aha! experience." It's like having a flash of insight which results in you realizing what the problem is or finding the solution to your problem. This has also been called the "eureka effect": You suddenly understand a previously unsolved or incomprehensible problem. All the patterns of the puzzle fall into place and you see just one pattern: "That's it. That is the problem or that's the solution."

Sixth step – Accommodate

What happens after that? You get cold feet. You say: "Yeah, but … however …" You accommodate. You say: "It's not exactly that, you see …" Like a baby, when it's born it needs to be washed. An idea, when it's born is the same: It's not perfect yet. It needs to be worked out to make it realistic. To understand it. We have to accommodate, to think of the "why nots." This is the step where you think: "Maybe I should wait. Maybe I should try another shop. I know the MacBook is the best computer available, but maybe it's too expensive." This is the step minutes before tying the knot, when the groom or the bride get cold feet. Maybe I am making a mistake. That is why in Jewish weddings they hold the groom from both sides holding his hands actually carrying him to the chuppa, the site where he will make his oath.

How should you accommodate your illumination, and handle your "cold feet" …

How can you manage this step? Take a piece of paper and divide it into three sections by drawing two horizontal lines across it. Label the upper section "Questions"; label the middle section "Doubts"; and label the lower section "Disagreements."

Questions, Doubts and Disagreements? What's the difference?

Let's look at some examples:

- Question: I am used to Windows laptops. Never had a Mac. Is it easy to transition from one operating system to the other?
- Doubt: I doubt it will work well. Hmmm, I am not sure.
- Disagreement: This will not work in practice.

In the Questions section, you are asking yourself for more details, more information. You might ask, for instance: "How will this aspect work?", "What is that?", etc. Questions are for clarification purposes.

If you are in doubt regarding the solution (or some aspect of it) list your concerns in the Doubts section. You don't need more information—you already have all the information you need—but you are not yet convinced your solution is going to work. Sometimes this uneasiness can manifest as a discomfort in our gut. You just don't feel right about the decision.

Disagreements means you really believe the solution is not going to work, and you know why.

Once you have written out all of your Questions, Doubts, and Disagreements:

- Take the list of questions and try to answer them one by one first until each has an answer.

- Change and adapt your diagnosis of the problem or the proposed solution as you deal with the questions, so that it's constantly evolving and growing—right in front of your eyes.

- When all of the questions have been answered, again accumulate Questions, Doubts, and Disagreements. The Doubts from the previous list will naturally move up to become Questions in the new list, and the Disagreements will move up to become Doubts. And you will start the process again. Again, deal only with the questions, until they are all answered.

- Next, do another QDD list. Watch as the Disagreements become Questions.

- Repeat the process until you have no more questions, doubts, or disagreements—until you see that they have all been dealt with.

Seventh step – Finalize

When we have cleared the questions, doubts and disagreements raised in the Accommodation step, we are ready to Finalize, which means … bite the bullet.

This brings us to the difference between decision-making and decision-taking.

Up to now, using the previous six steps, we were making the decision. Now we are ready for taking the decision. Move on. Done. Finished. To finalize your decision, you must have all four imperatives addressed: what, how, by when, and who.

Eighth step – Reinforcement

Is the decision-making process finished? The answer is no. There is one more step. You accommodated, you went through and cleared any qdd's, and you finalized your decision. There it is, your beautiful shiny stylish MacBook Air laptop. Then your friends come, and you proudly show them your new computer. "Oh …nice, you bought a new Mac …" "What do you think?" you ask them. Now, if they ask, "How much did you pay for it?" and upon hearing the price, they abruptly reply, "How much?? Are you crazy?" …

Notice what happened. You are past finalization, but where are your friends? They are starting the whole process from the beginning, accumulating .

Now: Are you really asking them what they think? Not at all. What are you really after? Reinforcement: "Please tell me I made a good decision. Tell me I bought the right computer. Tell me you love it as much as I do. Reinforce my decision."

And the (I)s look for ways to accept the decision.

How each PAEI style uses the 8 Step Decision-Making Process

Not everybody uses the 8 Step Decision-Making Process in the same way. Different PAEI styles advance through the decision-making process at a different pace.

This is what happens, typically, when a person needs to make some kind of decision:

First, there is no defreeze. You approach the issue in the middle of your hectic day. Instead of slowing down, defreezing, and taking a breath (to disassociate from the rush going on around you), you increase the rush: "C'mon, I have to decide on this. Move. There is no time."

Then, on top of this lack of defreeze, people of varying PAEI styles will begin to move differently across the eight steps.

An (A) person, for instance (a detail-oriented and overly organized bureaucrat type), will start out by accumulating information, and when he tries to deliberate that information, he will think: "Ahhh, I need more information." And more information. And even more. He will see the complexity of the problem and want to do a deep analysis, but will instead come down with "paralysis from over-analysis." For an (A) type, the end of an attempt to make a decision may look very similar to its beginning. Like nothing happened.

The next type, upon the slightest accumulation of information, will jump straight into Illumination. This type will say: "Aha! I know what I should do!" That's type (E). An (E) may jump too prematurely into illuminating without really understanding what the problem is (that is, without true prior accumulation and deliberation). And if another person accommodates their "solution" by telling them, "Perhaps this is not the best idea. Have you thought about this or that?" instead of adapting his idea based on this new advice or suggestion, an (E) might just move on to another idea. And another one. That's why, when it comes to decision-making, (E) s may have lots of ideas and illuminations, but they can end up confused over which decision to actually make.

And who hates this eight-step process with a passion? Every single accumulation, deliberation, and illumination step? That's the (P) type. He just wants to finalize and get out of there. "We are wasting our time, let's do something, we can worry about this later." They jump straight to the Seventh Step, Finalization. All of the previous steps are perceived as a waste of time. They just want to deal with the issue quickly and move on.

This, by the way, may explain many of the frictions that you as an individual may have with other people. Conflicts develop because of these differing speed preferences and the emphasis on the process of deciding. Arguments arise. And then the (I), will say: "C'mon, let's just listen to each other for a minute." (I)s want to make sure, oftentimes to a fault, that everyone is on board. That there is no conflict at all during a decision-making process and that we all agree one hundred percent. On an individual level, in their own decision-making, they want to reach a decision that makes them feel good. On a team or partner level, they want consensus. So where do they get stuck, in which step? In Step Six, Accommodation. They accommodate endlessly, as a way to avoid Finalization—because when we finalize, we are going to implement the decision, and that (if there is no perceived "feel-good" or total agreement on all sides), scares them. They want to make sure that nobody is "upset" with the decision, that everybody is happy.

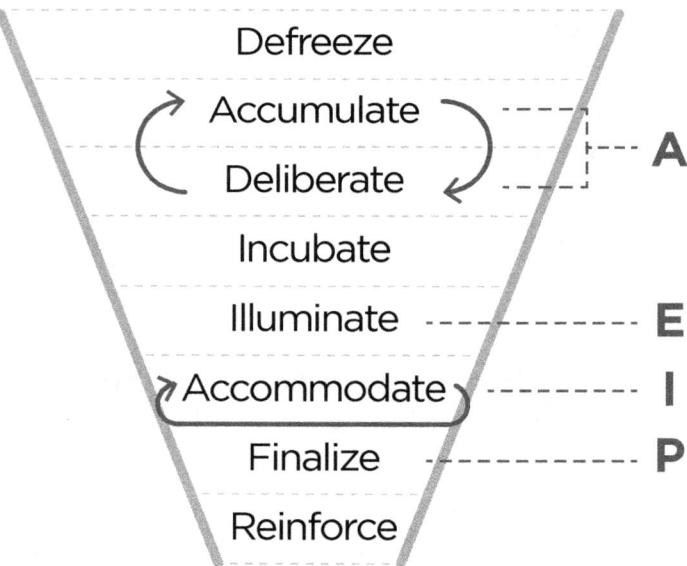

So let's summarize the main points for making, taking, and finalizing a decision:

- When faced with a problem, calm down. Defreeze. Give yourself some time, so that there is no rush.

- Next, on a piece of paper, write down all of the aspects of the problem. No discussion. No analysis. Just an accumulation of ideas or observations.

- Now look for a pattern. If you identify more than one pattern, try to see if they create an overall pattern. Can you put them into a sequence and does that reveal the grand pattern of what the problem is?

- Now ask yourself: "Do I have any questions, doubts, or disagreements pertaining to my illumination?"

- Answer any questions you may have and amend your conclusion as you go along. Continue answering questions until there are none left.

- By now you should have a defined problem with a solution that you can handle yourself.

- It's important to know how the different PAEI styles advance through the decision-making process, because people do not follow a road map. They do not defreeze, and they often try to make strategic decisions in a rush. If a coachee comes to me and says, "I have a major decision I need to make but I have very little time. I am in a rush." I will refuse to coach them on this. We must respect the importance of making a decision by giving it the amount of time it needs.

- Also, we might jump from *accumulate* to *illuminate*, and back to *accumulate*, and then *finalize* in haste and feel bad about our decision, and then start *illuminating* again …this creates a mess. It is always better to practice self-restraint and advance in an organized fashion. Do not start deliberating until you feel you have finished accumulating, etc.

- Understanding the criteria involved in making a decision—and how each PAEI type approaches the process—should help you as a coach later, when you are supporting a coachee and striving to keep them on track.

Foundational Tool #4:

The lens through which you see the world (perceptions of reality)

"We must look at the lens through which we see the world, as well as the world we see, and that the lens itself shapes how we interpret the world." —Stephen Covey

So far, we've seen that people of different PAEI styles behave differently. Guess what … they also think and perceive the world differently, as if they have different lenses through which they look at and interpret reality.

- There are three ways we can perceive reality:
- First, according to what **is** going on.
- Second, according to what we believe **should** be going on.

- Third, according to what we **want** to be going on.[13]

Let's illustrate this through an example.

You've just come home from the office after a long day, you grab something from the fridge, go to the living room, and open your laptop—with the intent to keep working until late in the evening. That's what is. This is the present reality.

But then, it crosses your mind that you have not spent much time with your family lately. You keep working, but in your mind the following thought pops up: "I should stop working and go play with the kids."

And maybe while all this is happening—you **are** sitting there working, while thinking that you **should** go play with your kids—you simultaneously know that what you really **want** to do is take off your shoes, throw yourself on the couch, and watch a movie on Netflix.

As you can see, when these three perceptions overlap, they can be a source of much frustration. They can create a lot of internal conflict between what you *are* doing versus what you believe you *should* be doing versus what you really *want* to be doing.

The problem, as you can begin to see, is that sometimes when you feel bad you might not be able to pinpoint why. Because all of this "internal noise" can go in the back of your mind, just beyond your awareness, without you even realizing it. An important first step in Adizes Coaching is to bring this *is/want/should* lens into awareness …to help you recognize how your mind is working …so you can take control of it.

---

13. The perceptions of reality as presented can be related to Sigmund Freud's psychoanalytic theory: Is relates to the id, want to the ego, and should to the super-ego.

"The range of what we think and do is limited by what we fail to notice. And because we fail to notice that we fail to notice, there is little we can do to change; until we notice how failing to notice shapes our thoughts and deeds." —R. D. Laing

To make it even more interesting, you can perceive a situation not only from three different perceptions—is, want, or should—but also from any combination of these perceptions. If you look at the diagram below, you'll see three circles labeled *is*, *want*, and *should*.

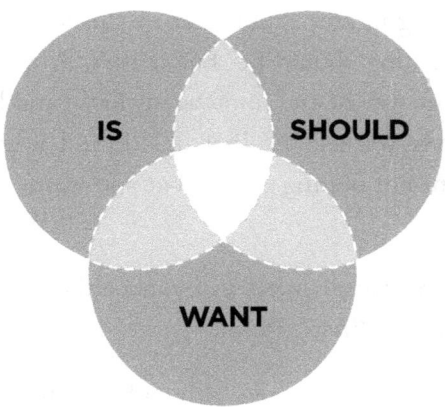

When we study the overlapping elements, it gets really fascinating. Allow me to number the common areas between each pair of perceptions as 1, 2, and 3, and call the space where all three of the perceptions overlap "mine."

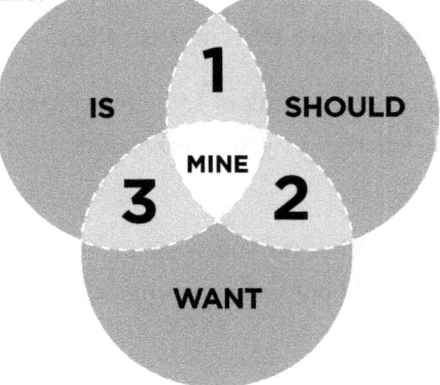

What's happening in the area marked as number 1? Let's look at a marriage, as an example. In this area something is going on in your marriage, something should be going on, but you don't want it! This is called: I am staying in this marriage and I should, because of the children, although I really don't want to be married to my spouse. You are denying yourself your needs. You are choosing to do what you perceive should be done to fulfil your children's needs. You are a good person. You believe this is the right thing to do and that's why you should do it, although you don't want to do it.

What is happening in area number 2? In this area, you want something, and something should be, but it isn't. A typical example of this: I want to lose weight and improve my looks and I should because my doctor already warned me that if I don't I might become diabetic…, but I am not dieting… So what you want, should be, but it isn't happening.

In area number 3, you do what you want although you realize you should not. I call this "living in sin."

For example: I consciously smoke although I realize I should not. So why do I do it? Because I want to. I don't care. Notice the difference here with the previous example, where I actually didn't want to break the diet. Here I do want to smoke, and I actually don't care about the consequences, about the should not.

All areas except the core are areas of frustration.

To understand this better, think of some frustrations you have in any area of your life, whether in your work/career, your family/relationships, or your health.

Now classify them: What do you want or not want? What do you believe should or should not be happening? Compare these to what is or is not happening.

What happens at the center area where the three circles overlap? That is where what is going on, what should be going on, and what you want to be going on overlap. What is this area called? "Mine." Let me explain:

Many years ago, when my child was still a toddler in his high chair, banging a teaspoon on his tray, he pointed to something on the table and uttered one of his first words, "Mine." I was puzzled. I didn't understand. How could he have developed this proprietary idea of "ownership" so early in his life? I told him, "It's not yours." He carried on: "Miiiiine!!!!" Around this same time, I heard a comedy album by comedian Bill Cosby in which he described his children, who also shouted "Mine!" all the time. Lecturing all over the world, wherever I went, I asked people: "Did your kids shout "mine" when they were very young?" And I was invariably told, "Yes!" (in every conceivable language). I was still puzzled: How could that be? Why would one of the first words uttered by a child be the word "mine"?

I believe that when we are very young, is, want, and should overlap. They are one in the same. When you are a toddler, there is no real distinction between what is, what should be, and what you want. It's all the same to you. So mine doesn't really mean "proprietary." What the child means is, "I want it. And since I want it, it is mine." There is no should for a toddler. The should is a learned perception. It comes from experiences or socialization that a toddler does not yet have.

What happens as we grow and progress along our lifecycle? (See Tool #5 for a full description of each lifecycle stage.) The circles of perception start to separate into three, distinct circles. Suddenly, the child begins to understand that there is a difference between the is, the want, and the should. And that's why little kids cry a lot. They are beginning to realize the differences: What they want is not necessarily what should be and not necessarily what is (and not necessarily what they are going to get). Say to a toddler, "Do not touch this kettle. It is hot." What is he going to do as soon as you turn your back?

He is going to touch it and begin to realize that in life what **is** you might not want to or you should not do it …he will begin to feel the pain.

Consider, for instance, an interaction with your child, such as the following:

Parent: Go to bed. IT IS already nine o'clock.
Child: But I don't WANT to.
Parent: But you SHOULD, IT IS late …
Child: But I don't WANT to.
Parent: Go to sleep!!! Now!!!
Child: (Starts crying.)

The child begins to realize and learn something about life: What I want, I shouldn't always want. And what I should do, I do not always want to do. All of these experiences cause pain. So little children cry … a lot.

We would all continue crying for the rest of our lives, except, as we grow older we learn how to hide our tears. What is, we often don't want; and what we want, often, we shouldn't have; and what should be, often isn't. That's called life.

HOW EACH PAEI STYLE PERCEIVES REALITY

Interestingly, the is/want/should lenses operate differently in each of the PAEI styles. Facing the same objective situation, an (E) person will perceive reality very differently from an (A) person. Same reality, different interpretation. That's because each one is operating from a completely different frame of mind, and a completely different "filter" of reality. Just as if they were each wearing glasses with different colored lenses. While (E) might be seeing and perceiving the world through blue lenses, (A) might be seeing and perceiving the world through yellow lenses.

Some types see the world from the "want" perspective. In any given situation, their first thought is: "What is it that I want from this situation?" Others come from a should perspective: "Ok, so this is the situation. What should I do here? What would be the correct thing to do?" This may come from their own morals, or the teachings they received from their parents or community while growing up. And yet others will perceive a situation strictly from what needs to be done regardless of what they want or believe should be done.

Which of the PAEI types comes from the "want" circle? Since I want it, it should be, and it better be. Who are they? They are the (E) types. These are the people you know who have remained childish despite their age—they behave like spoiled children. They insist on the "want" even if it is a "should not" or an "is not" …

"I always knew what I wanted. Can't understand those people who don't know what they want and follow others' agenda. Bureaucrats who do what they are told. I put myself first. I call it "Me, Inc." Find what is it that you want and go get it. Don't let anyone step in your way. Because no one is gonna get it for you." —Gene Simmons

What type comes from the should angle? "Since it should be, that's what I want. I want what should be done." Should is the driving force. This is the classic (A) type: the detailed, dutiful, thorough, risk-averse person. We do what we should do. We're good soldiers. What do we want? Never mind that. We focus on what we should do.

"Whether you like it or not, you have a moral obligation to care for those in need." —Desmond Tutu

And who comes from the is perception? "Never mind what we want, or what we should do. Common …let us just do it!" Whatever needs to be done. "What should we do? It doesn't matter, just do it!!!" This is the (P) type.

> *"If you spend too much time thinking about a thing,*
> *you'll never get it done."* —Bruce Lee

And finally, the (I) type, looks for the "mine" for the decision that all agree to. The (I) type is accommodating, has no bias of his own, does not care what is, should or is wanted as long as there is an agreement.

"You win the victory when you yield to friends." —Sophocles

We really need to pay attention to the words we use. "All people are born equal" is a great example. Are all people really born equal? Or are we saying that they should be born equal? Or that we want them to be born equal? For personal growth, it's critical that we continually examine the lenses we use in our personal and professional lives, as well as the lenses our coachees use.

Perceiving reality is important for coaching because people use the word should when they mean want. Or they want something but disregard the is (reality).

The sequence we should all follow, and that you should guide your coachees to follow, is:[14]

Start with reality first : what IS going on. In light of it, define what do you WANT to do. Once you are clear with that, SHOULD you do it? What is the cost-value relationship? Now you are ready to finalize the decision.

---

14. See Part 5 of this book for a more in-depth discussion of this sequence.

Foundational Tool #5:

The lifecycle of the individual

Every living organism has a lifecycle. Whether it is a plant, an animal, a human being, or an organization—all are born, grow, age, and die.

As individuals, we change and progress along a lifecycle, following predictable patterns of behavior. At each stage, we manifest certain struggles, certain difficulties, or transitional problems that we must overcome. Sometimes we successfully solve the issues we encounter on our own, and other times we require external help. Because the problems that arise throughout a given lifecycle change at each stage, the coaching being given also needs to adapt and be tailored specifically to the particular stage that a problem is occurring in. What works and is appropriate at one stage won't necessarily work or be appropriate for another. This contingency consideration sets apart Adizes from every other coaching approach.

The stages of the human lifecycle are:[15]

---

15. The human lifecycle is derived from the theory of corporate lifecycles, see Adizes I.: *Managing Corporate Lifecycles*: An updated and expanded look at the

1. Newly-born
2. Infancy
3. Adolescence
4. Prime
5. Middle Age
6. Old Age
7. Falling Apart
8. Death

The following diagram illustrates the stages along the lifecycle curve.

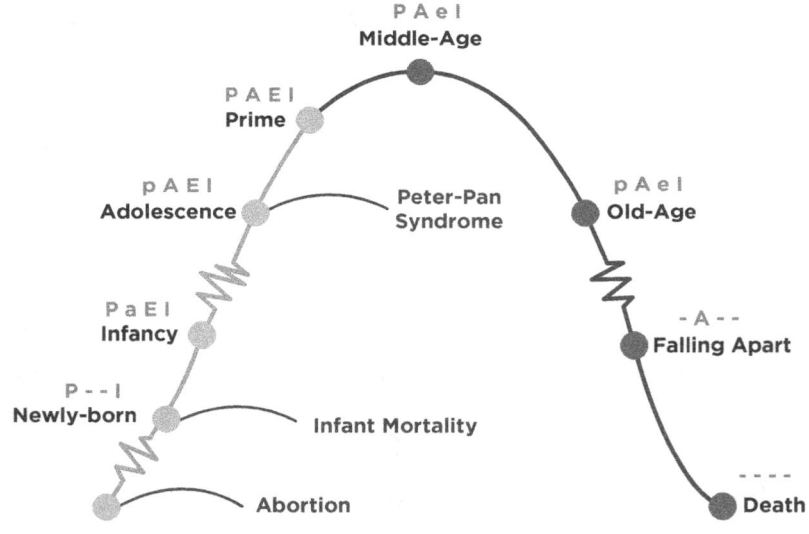

At each stage in the lifecycle, a specific (PAEI) role needs to be developed. It's as though the system naturally develops the roles in a

---

Corporate Lifecycles, first printing: Paramus, NJ: Prentice Hall Press, 1999. Revised Edition 2004. Reprinted by Adizes Institute Publications https://publications.adizes.com

certain sequence. The roles develop experientially, which is manifested in the behavior of the person.

If a person at a particular stage struggles to develop a certain role or roles, then certain problems can typically be expected. The problems are impacted by which role is developing and where the person is in their lifecycle.

Problems that are normal, and to be expected at one stage of the lifecycle, if not treated properly, can become abnormal at the next stage of the lifecycle, and even critical if allowed to continue into another stage. In other words, some problems are normal, and actually part of the struggle to develop a certain role or roles, in order to move to the next stage on the lifecycle; but abnormal problems are when, repetitively, a role doesn't develop.

Notice that the roles follow a pattern of interplay, development, and eventually deterioration—this is what creates how an individual behaves over its lifecycle.

If an individual is able to perform all four roles above threshold, then the individual will be functional, well-rounded, and healthy. They will, however, always have normal problems to overcome as a role is developing, moving into the growing stages, and being maintained (so it does not atrophy), when it reaches the aging stages of the lifecycle.

If the individual is missing one or more roles—and therefore not developing every subsystem—problems will become abnormal and the individual, as a system, will become dysfunctional and manifest symptoms of stress and disintegration.

Now let's go deeper into each stage and see what happens as the lifecycle progresses. Notice, though, how the cycle begins with the initial evolution of the individual as a baby, and continues all the way to maturity, then aging, and finally dying. Note that the coaching methodology can be applied from adolescence on.[16]

THE GROWING STAGES

Newly born: P--I

When babies are born, life in the outside world begins. Out of the protected environment of the womb, they now enter into life. They are completely dependent on others for survival, with crying as their only means of communication. From their parents, they desperately need the love of the (I) role (kindness, gentleness, calm, understanding), and the care of the (P) role (feeding, bathing), to grow normally. They cry and sleep in their parents' room, who dutifully wake up in the middle of the night to make sure they are okay, and to feed them as much and as many times as they need.

In this stage, the (P) and (I) roles are dominant. This can be seen as the baby puts everything in its mouth, and food is the driving force for his or her behavior.

This stage becomes unhealthy if a child is underfed (parent with (P) deficiency), or unloved (parent with (I) deficiency), or if one or both parents mistreats the child in some way, or the child suffers trauma due to circumstances of their environment—such as being born in a war zone.

Kids cry a lot. They most often cry because they want something. Initially, crying is their only means of communication. The

---

16. **Life coaching for kids**—a rapidly developing field under the larger umbrella of life coaching—can highly benefit from several of the Adizes tools and methods presented in this book, which can be adapted to be used from elementary school age on. It can be highly beneficial, for instance, to teach Adizes tools (such as PAEI) to kids. The Adizes Institute has a division where nursery teachers are trained to teach children the PAEI roles and styles and make them aware of how they are behaving. Children learn to become aware and critical from early age.

perception of want dominates their behavior. There is no should and the IS is ignored. I cry because I want. Period.

If a parent does not properly handle the strain of a crying baby (who is merely trying to get a need met), then the child's should or is will not fully develop. This experience will impact the child's behavior later on in life.

For example: A baby cries constantly because he wants to be held. He refuses to stay on his own in his carriage.

If the parent yields, the baby perceives that nonstop crying is the correct way to get what he or she wants. So not only does the PAEI behavior change as a person grows and evolves, so does the sequence of perceptions. It starts with want. Alongside want, the should is also emerging. In turn, the IS is also in the beginning stages of being learned. If you say to a toddler, "Don't touch the stove, it IS hot." and then turn your back for a second, what will the toddler do? He will touch the stove, burn himself, and learn. What he wanted (to touch the stove) was not a good thing to want, and thus, the should now appears in his perception: "I should not touch the stove, even if I want to, because the stove is hot and I will be burned. I should stay away from the stove."

Infancy: P a E I

Toddler age. Now the (E) role develops quickly. The infant displays enormous amounts of energy and in no time will begin to crawl and walk. Everything looks interesting. The toddler explores everything, opening every possible drawer. Everything has to be "tested." The faster the (E) develops the more the parents need to watch and be vigilant, because the toddler is all (P) and (E) without any awareness of safety.

This lack of awareness and regard for safety may lead to things like falling off the couch or putting unsafe things in his or her mouth. The child is taking in his or her environment and learning at an accelerated rate—literally seeing the world for the first time. The (I) role is permanent, it does not develop, it is innate. The child seeks opportunities to play and interact with others. If there are siblings, sometimes they fulfill this immediate need. The parents get down on the floor to play, or take the child to the park—fulfilling the child's need for love, connection, and human interaction.

The playfulness, creativity, vitality, ingenuity, and imagination that are seen at this stage are all (E) components. It's (E) in its purer form and that's why we talk about "seeing the world through the eyes of a child." There is a unique beauty and simplicity to it.

> *"Until one looks back on one's own past one fails to realize what an extraordinary view of the world a child has."* —Agatha Christie

It's at this Go-Go stage when our environment (mainly home and/or school) socializes us and begins to teach us (A). You can't teach rules to a newborn, but as soon as a child is crawling and gets too close to the oven or becomes curious about electrical wires, the parents begin to teach limits. The (A) role begins to emerge and is further refined when the child starts preschool and is taught to how put things in their place, how to behave, how to go to sleep at night, etc. The child hears the word "no" a lot. As this lifecycle stage progresses, and there is a transition from early to mid to late childhood, the limitations begin to appear not only from (A) concerns for safety ("Beware of the stove!"), but also from (I) concerns for behavior ("That's not a proper way to talk to your mother!"), and even (AI) concerns for proper socialization ("Who's that you were playing with? I don't think he's a good influence."). Kids begin to be taught (and learn) the rules of being a proper and acceptable member of society.

How a child responds to the process of socialization—whether it is administered with love (I) or without—will have a huge impact on the success of the upcoming stage, Adolescence. It's here that—if they were fortunate enough—their parents knew how to perform the art of correcting while connecting, of balancing limits (A) with love (I), of socializing without making their child feel unwanted or ashamed. Research shows that individuals who report having had a happy childhood also typically report having grown up with parents who were neither too permissive nor too strict—who were good at enforcing limits and being firm, while still conveying the message that they loved their children.

Normal problems during this stage include: resistance to rules; failure to respond to discipline; scenes at food and meal times; displays of frustration, anger, and other strong emotions; rivalry with siblings; struggles with studies and/or school authorities; difficulty balancing entertainment and school (too much internet, videogames, etc.); occasional fights with other kids. All seem problems caused by the the struggle to develop (A) without losing (I).

Abnormal problems that might be seen during this stage: withdrawing for long periods of time or preferring to be alone most of the time; inability to make friends after a reasonable period; addiction to entertainment, videogames, etc. (to the point of developing an inability to study, or focus, or keep up with basic hygiene, or becoming obese); self-injuring behaviors. The abnormality seems to be caused by a complete lack of (A), and it will be very difficult to implant (A) later on in adolescence if the foundation for (A) was not established early on.

Within the child's perception, the want still dominates but the should is emerging and being developed—as well as the IS, which is the acceptance of reality.

Adolescence: p A E i

The onset of puberty brings forth a series of biological, physical, and emotional events that cause, for several years, a serious misalignment of the subsystems. The physical subsystem begins to transform rapidly into an adult body, while the mental/biological and emotional subsystems enter into turmoil and develop much more slowly.

This is when an adolescent's external environment begins to say: "You are not a little kid anymore," and a demand for a different kind of behavior appears, such as the following of more complex rules (A). The problem, however, is that the individual is still not an adult; and as research shows, while the body will mature physically in adolescence, the brain will continue to develop for some years (sometimes until the mid-twenties). The more misalignment of subsystems you have, the more problems you are likely to have.

In the Adizes Methodology, another name for this stage is "Turbulence." It is at this point in the lifecycle when the person needs to learn the (A) role—which until now has been weak, with much allowance for transgressions—but now, in adolescence (in preparation for adult life), there is suddenly a need to internalize the societal rules of coexistence. It's not possible to do as they wish all the time. However, the problem is that adolescents must learn (A) while dealing with hormonal upheavals and their search for an identity, so intrapersonal (I) is in agitation, too. (That's why mood swings are so common at this stage.)

Part of the problem is that the teenager is wanting a higher level of authority, similar to that of an adult, but is still only capable of handling the responsibility of a child. This is the stage where (A) and (E) are in conflict the most. On one hand the young adolescent wants to maintain his or her (E) (i.e., trying many different "looks" to find what suits them); they want to discover the image that they will carry on into adulthood. The (E) role can also manifest in risky behaviors. The problem is that if the (P) role is strong and propels them into risky behaviors, while the (A) role is not sufficiently developed enough to unleash restraint, then the adolescent is more likely to partake in actions that may have a negative impact on their future. This short-term recklessness can happen because the cognitive ability to consider the long-term implications of their actions is still developing in the teen brain. Adolescents in this stage of development are sometimes referred to as having "a Ferrari engine with bicycle breaks."

Today, with external (E) media bombardment reaching new heights, it's no easy task for teens to navigate the adolescence stage. From the context of peer pressure, and with bullying and online shaming in the rise, they need to form their identity and build their self-esteem more quickly and solidly than ever before. What can really support them along the way is the love that they feel from their immediate environment, especially from their parents. In other words, the foundation of the (I) role, how securely it was built, and how well it is still maintained around them is the key to supporting them at this stage. If they were lucky enough to grow up with mature and loving parents, they may still have difficulty absorbing the new (A) limitations, but they will have a far easier time than in cases where (I) is missing. A low or missing (I) creates the most conducive environment to stereotypical teen rebellion. The lower the (I), the stronger the rebellion and its manifestations will be.

In addition, when interpersonal (I) is low, mutual trust and respect (MT&R) is also low, which can often result in a teen omitting facts or lying directly to their parents. Most teens, in developing privacy, become somewhat secretive, because they don't want their parents involved in every decision. But the less (I) there is, the less they trust and respect their parents—typically because a human being cannot live without (I). They will develop MT&R with their friends (or worse, a gang) instead of with their moms and/or[17] dads.

17. In an ideal scenario, the parents work as a complementary team, providing a balanced parenting style. But this is not always the case, and sometimes only one parent can provide the (I) role. Hence the importance of the "and/or" distinction here, because the parent providing the (I) can at least act as the communication channel with the teen, which is a better scenario than no (I) at all. These are the cases in which the teen rebellion takes place, and all the anger is directed toward the "disciplining" (A) parent, while the (I) parent functions as the more supporting one with the teen.

Low MT&R ends up lowering self-trust and self-respect, causing confusion and a lot of noise between the teen's ears, sometimes for years to come. This troubles teens as they search for an identity and self-esteem.

Why is this information critical for coaching teenagers? Because it helps us to understand problems that are considered normal during this stage, as well as those that should be considered abnormal:

Normal problems during this stage include: emotional friction with parents and authority figures regarding limits, resistance to (A) rules, confusion, identity crises, moodiness, exaggerated reactions, dating drama, peer pressure, academic stress and other ups and downs at school, and excessive use of electronics and the internet.

Abnormal problems during this stage include: delinquency and criminal activity, gang affiliation, risky behavior (such as drinking and driving), addictions (from alcohol and drugs to the internet), depression, bullying, pregnancy and sexually-related problems, self-harm, eating disorders (pervasive mostly in female teens, e.g., anorexia, bulimia, or binge eating).

An interesting phenomenon is happening in our Western culture today, with what is known as "Peter Pan Syndrome." In the portion of the lifecycle diagram, below, this phenomenon is represented by an exit from the curve at the point of adolescence and into a "stuckness" point.

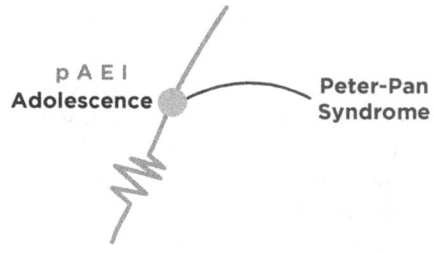

The syndrome refers to the inability of an individual to transition healthily out of the Adolescent stage. The person, already an adult physically, remains unable to align his or her emotional and mental subsystems, and continues to cling to the carefree life of childhood. This results in an incomplete adolescence, as this stage has failed to create the (A) role. The individual is unable to make commitments and finds emotional and financial obligations too difficult. In turn, this impacts the ability to become a fully functional adult, and renders him or her incapable of entering into a long-term relationship (I), both of which require commitment and a threshold level of maturity. This type of person may spend money unwisely and "live for today"—another sign they haven't fully developed an ability to invest in their actions and/or foresee long-term consequences. A pattern of immaturity may develop in their working life, too, as they may feel tempted to leave a job as soon as it becomes boring or requires considerable effort (P). It's as if the inability to successfully incorporate the (A) role during adolescence now begins to take a toll, eroding the rest of the PAEI roles.

This is the stage in which the perception of should should come fully into play, as they learn to subdue the want that has thus far dominated their life, and yield to the should while recognizing the reality of what is.

Prime: P A E I18

What is Prime? It's the optimal condition in the lifecycle, where the individual can finally achieve balance due to the properly developed

18.   When we denote the Prime stage as having a PAEI code (all capital letters), we do not intend to say that an individual becomes "perfect" in Prime. What it means instead is that no role is missing when the person reaches Prime, and they are at a level that in Adizes theory is called "self-leadership", meaning: in addition to having no blanks in the PAEI code, the individual has the (I) role plus another vitamin (P, A or E) also at capital level. Thus, different people arrive to Prime differently, according to their own style. A person who has a dominant (P) orientation, for instance, arrives to Prime as PaeI. Prime means all PAEI roles have

presence of the (E) and (A) vitamins, and without losing (I). This is made possible because the development of (A) has triggered a process through which the person has successfully finalized their identity formation and built up enough self-esteem (high self-trust and self-respect).

If an individual successfully develops the (A) role during adolescence, without losing (E), then he or she can enter Prime. The incorporation of (A) functions as a catalyst to align the previously misaligned subsystems and the person transitions into a healthy adulthood.

The (A) vitamin triggers emotional maturity, so through (A) the emotional subsystem gets aligned. As a result, emotional reactions are more appropriate, less dramatic, and more like responses than reactions. The individual, with high self-esteem, is healthily independent. (A) has helped to remove childish notions from the mind, which has allowed the individual to get more realistic about life. So in Prime, the emotional and mental/logical subsystems finally catch up with the body and the individual becomes "together." Glued.

Without losing (E), there is a consolidation of the personal long-term vision. A vision that inspires and prompts us to keep learning, growing, loving, and serving. While fully vibrant and active on the outside, a certain feeling of plenitude and peace (that has never been felt before), arises on the inside.

> *"Maturity starts when drama ends."*   —Anonymous

In Prime, the person is fun to be with. No longer an adolescent, they are a flexible, fresh person, full of (E), who is capable of taking on adult responsibilities and obligations (A). They have learned to enjoy life, but without being reckless—and have learned to be in the moment, but without sacrificing the future. This person is in an optimal

---

been developed and the person is capable to perform any of the roles if the situation calls for it (not simultanelusly though, but over time and different situations).

state for a relationship, because he or she cannot only be loving but is also able to commit. The Prime individual is functional and flexible, with a good awareness of their available strengths and resources—as well as their weaknesses and opportunities for growth—and is neither afraid of admitting a mistake, nor of putting in the hard work (whether investing in a career or in a long-term relationship).

In the previous stages, a lot of energy was wasted on internal conflict. Remember the confusion surrounding identity in adolescence? That energy has now been liberated and can be channeled into constructive purposes. A person in Prime is continuously learning and growing. He or she is always looking for new sources of education and ways to contribute to the lives of others.

Are there problems in Prime? You bet. Life continues and as long as there is life, there is change, and as long as there is change there will be problems. But because all four roles have adequately developed along the lifecycle thus far, in Prime a person has the ability to adapt to new situations by calling upon elements of the appropriate PAEI style in any given moment.

Staying in versus sliding out of Prime

As we have previously shown, the (E) and (A) roles are incompatible. They engage in a constant "struggle," periodically exchanging dominance. Sometimes an individual is more flexible than controllable, and other times he is not flexible enough—becoming either too conservative and formal, or too expansive and excitable.

As we age our body starts falling apart as different organs have different life spans. When that happens the fixed energy has to be dedicated to the pains and strugles of aging and a person feels less and less energy. Havng reduced energy impacts a persons behavior. They turn more to the (A) role to increase the efficient behhavior they need now. They develop routines and refuse change like moving their home somewhere else although their neighborhoid is becoming dangerous to live in.

The struggle can end up with form taking over: controllability over flexibility. When this happens, the person starts to age, behaviorally speaking. The habits of order that took effort to introduce in adolescence can now become the driving force. The individual arranges their life into one of greater predictability, with routine as the main characteristic. When (A) takes control over (E), behavior becomes more rigid and structured, more oriented toward order, and the excitement and passion found in the earlier stages begins to go down.

Research done in the field of coaching has found that, from this point on, two types of aging typically occur, manifested into two distinctive attitudes:

1. **Those who keep learning and contributing, and never seem to get bored.** These are the people that, in spite of their old age, remain active and curious and seem to be able to continually provide themselves with stimulating activities. They still have their (E).

2. **Those who stop learning, become passive, and seem bored, as if not knowing what to do anymore.** They just sit and stare off into space. No more ideas. No more excitement. Just boring routines. They spend their time in front of a TV, zapping the channels, idly passing the moments.

The cause of behavioral aging is the loss of (E).

(E) is lost when a person doesn't feel the challenges in front of them are worth putting energy into, they don't feel needed anymore, they have retired or lost their job or business, or their children have left home.

Behavioral aging can happen to a young person too. A person can exhibit symptoms of example number two, above, at a very young age.

They may feel impotent and bored. This type of aging is not dependent on chronological age.

In my book "Managing Corporate Lifecycles,"[19] I wrote:

> *"The more an organization perceives it's empowered to solve its problems, the younger it is,"* and *"Once it starts perceiving itself as impotent, it starts to age. It's old when it perceives itself as powerless, as if destiny had taken charge."*

This is true not only for organizations, but for individuals as well.

In coaching there is a distinction between a "fixed mindset" and a "growth mindset." And the secret to staying young in spite of age (in other words, staying in Prime) is to adopt the latter approach. Let me explain:

1. **Coachees with an "aging" or "fixed" mindset typically dislike challenges and therefore avoid them or easily give up on them.** They believe intelligence is static. They are more pessimistic, dislike negative feedback (even if it is useful), and see most efforts as fruitless or worse. As a result, they may plateau early, never achieving their full potential. They may have a deterministic view of the world and look, think, and act conservatively, even from a young chronological age. In my experience with coaching this type of client, there is a higher correlation with (A) in their personality style.

2. **Coachees with a "young" growth mindset typically embrace challenges (regardless of chronological age), are very expansive, and believe that intelligence is not fixed, but rather, can be developed.** This leads to a desire to learn. They

---

19. Adizes, I.: Managing Corporate Lifecycles: An updated and expanded look at the Corporate Lifecycles. First printing, Paramus, NJ: Prentice Hall Press, 1999. Reprinted and available from Adizes Institute Publications at https://publications.adizes.com

persist in the face of setbacks (when there is enough (P), that is), see effort as the path to mastery, look for the lessons in everything that happens, and as a result, they have a greater chance to reach an ever-higher level of achievement. All this gives them a greater sense of free will (in contrast to the determinism of an aging mentality). In my experience with coaching this type of client, there is a higher correlation with (E) in their personality style.

Dr. Eric Lenze, Professor of Psychiatry at Washington University and a specialist on elderly boredom, says that "In old age, boredom is detrimental for old people's health."

So what is the good news in light of the above? It is simply this: With proper maintenance of the (E) vitamin, a person can stay in Prime and avoid behavioral aging. Although the body continues to age naturally and chronologically, an individual does not have to age behaviorally. One can stay in Prime until death and even that is not necessarily the end. If the descendants, friends, or even students of a person carry on his or her legacy, the individual's spirit will continue to make contributions, even after the physical body dies.

The main difference is the existence of, or the lack of, (E).

And the proper dosage of (E), toward off boredom, needs to be accompanied by a healthy dose of (I): To stay in Prime a person must not only continue to learn, but also continue to be involved in social and interpersonal endeavors. In other words, they must continue to do good and contribute their experience and wisdom to the world. In Prime there is an alignment of the spiritual subsystem, as well. (E) without (I) is barren.

With a large intrapersonal and interpersonal (I) (which needs to be nourished continually), and (E) (whereby the person is involved long-term in learning and continuing to grow emotionally and intellectually), a person can stay in Prime much longer than anybody else of his or her chronological age.

In Prime is, want, and should are handled in the right sequence. It all starts with is. A person in Prime has dreams (want) but understands the limitations of their dreams (should) because they have a good grasp of reality (is). Based on that it brings the want into the process of decision-making and then curtails the want to fit the should.

THE AGING STAGES

Middle Age: P A e I

In a world of accelerating change, it's not easy to keep up with all that is going on, and inevitably, in a culture that glorifies youth, a feeling of aging may kick in. The (A), which was first introduced in adolescence, begins to subtly take over and shape life. In a world driven by technological innovation (E), it's becoming increasingly difficult to "catch up" with change. And seeing those around us naturally adopt new technologies can make a person feel old.

Aging, then, is synonymous with losing (E).

This stage can be triggered by chronological age, as the passing of time brings on physical aging. It also brings, sooner or later, the aging or death of our parents (and with that, the recognition of one's own mortality). It can also bring, without notice, various types of crises in any number of areas in an individual's personal or professional lives.

Often, this aging process is conducive to a period of reflecting back on life's achievements (or lack thereof/regrets) in work or career, and in family relationships.

This all, of course, sounds quite dooming, but remember: The aging stages do not have to happen. A person can stay in Prime if rejuvenation measures (E) are taken.

Old Age: p A e I

In aging, the should becomes dominant. The want and the is are ignored or at best not playing a major role on behavior.

To retard aging do not let the (E) to atrophy. Simply put, continuing to be curious and having a fresh approach toward life. Believing that it's still possible to solve problems, that there is still potency and agency and power. If an individual doesn't succeed and instead becomes more increasingly settled in (A), aging accelerates. A conservative sense and a tendency to repeat the old and stop processing the new will kick in. In other words, the learning process will stop. And with that will come an attitude that destiny has taken charge. The individual will perceive himself or herself as powerless, as impotent.

As said above, the more a person perceives themselves as empowered to solve his or her own problems, the younger he or she will be.

At this stage some people attempt to use artificial measures as a substitute for the missing (E) vitamin. Suddenly there is a shift. A fifty-year-old individual begins to wear ripped jeans and rock concert T-shirts, just as he or she did in adolescence. Others get a face-lift or inject Botox in what seems to be an uphill battle against aging. And still others trade in the family car for a zippy cabriolet. Beyond aesthetics, often this is driven by a fear of aging and a desperate attempt to battle it externally.

What individuals at this stage fail to learn is that for humans, aging doesn't start with white hair or wrinkles. Even the middle-age spread of a person's midsection is not the real start of aging. Aging starts in the mind, when an individual gets lazier and lazier about initiating "newness" in their life and then, eventually, stops responding to change. Remember that the (E) vitamin is all about responding to or initiating change, but at this stage there is a sudden drop in this vitamin.

Some attempt to inject (E) externally by pursuing a relationship with a younger woman or man. Similar to an aging company that buys a start-up in an attempt to rejuvenate its own culture, many individuals try to rejuvenate themselves through another person.

Falling Apart: - A - -

The slide into the Falling Apart phase of the lifecycle is subtle. A traditionalist person, having failed to inject (E), becomes even more locked into a stable and rigid routine, and aging now becomes part of his or her identity. A certain bitterness may kick in. What characterizes Autopilot, however, is ongoing boredom, resulting from an accumulated lack of (E) and a slowing down in the person's routines. Life becomes more "waiting to die" than "being of service" and feeling truly alive. The person just goes through the motions.

As the body starts to disintegrate, it uses more and more of the limited fixed energy that is required to keep it functioning. Thus with aging there is a feeling of less and less energy. As the person tires more easily with that lower energy, he or she is less prone to initiate new projects or innovations that require energy.

And as the body is falling apart, more and more it needs to rely on external intervention to make it function—thus causing mechanistic integration and interdependency (A). This is manifested in frequent visits to doctors, in an attempt to help the body continue operating its growing stages and the internal body mechanisms that used to do the job so well (I). A physically younger body can continually recuperate and recover. Not true for old age.

In this stage, what is the dominant perception? IS. Realization of reality. Based on that, the decision now emerges to rely on should. The want has faded.

The sequence of perceptions along the lifecycle curve are: the want of childhood shifts to the should (which starts strongly in adolescence and is in full bloom in middle age), which shifts to the is in older age (as an individual accepts reality and stops dreaming or even showing interest in the course of daily life).

The individual finally reaches the last stage in the lifecycle, Death, when the physical and emotional behavioral body stop functioning altogether (- - - -).

Is It Possible to Avoid Aging and Stay in Prime?

This lifecycle is not inevitable. A person can achieve Prime and stay in Prime until physical death. It's not necessary to go through all the pains described at every stage of the lifecycle. An individual can advance to Prime fast and well with just a little of the pain that we have described here.

What does this advancement depend on? First, the existence (or lack) of the four PAEI vitamins. This is a must. Without the four PAEI roles it is virtually impossible to become a healthy individual. It will be impossible to align the four human subsystems. The person will simply be dysfunctional. Second, the creation and nurturing of[20] self-trust and self-respect. Moreover, in Prime one also achieves self-acceptance, self-love, and self-care.

How can this behavior be achieved and how can we help others achieve it as well? This is what the remainder of this book is about. Having dedicated Part 2 to describing the foundational arsenal of Adizes tools for Personal Growth, in Parts 3 and 4 we will explore

---

20.   I have been writing this book at the age of 84.

the coaching framework for creating change and personal growth for oneself and others.

Part 3:

Self-coaching – "First, grow yourself" – The Adizes Systemic Coaching Framework

"You will accomplish much more, much more easily if you take the time to first strengthen your personal foundation." —Thomas Leonard

How can we improve the quality of our lives with Adizes? How can we achieve higher levels of self-trust and self-respect, become whole, and get our act together? What can we do on a daily basis to become more effective and efficient as individuals? In this part of the book we'll dive deep into self-coaching with the Adizes Methodology.

Why is this important? Because everything in this world is dynamic and changing, and change causes disintegration. Nothing stays the same, and if you are not actively growing as a human being, you are declining in some way. When disintegrating, you suffer and make other people suffer. Disintegration drains your energy.

Conversely, when you actively integrate the different parts of yourself, you become whole and full of energy and vitality. You grow, which allows you to contribute to others. The way to share your gifts with the world is by growing yourself first; hence, the importance of internal integration in the Adizes Methodology.

This part of the book is divided into two big sections: In the first section, Adizes for First-Order Change, it will be presented how to self-coach when working on relatively simple, short-term goals. In the second section, Adizes for Second-Order Change, you will be guided through the protocols for dealing with more complex problems.

ADIZES FOR FIRST-ORDER OF CHANGE

If you have a problem, the Adizes tools can help you to self-coach and quickly produce a first-order change. These techniques work well for healthy, functional people who need help managing daily challenges that can be addressed without the external intervention. This is a result-oriented process that can be highly effective and efficient, as it starts with a self-diagnosis that cuts through the noise and helps you to quickly focus on what matters in order to obtain a desired result.

Note that in first-order change, the relative size of your PAEI code doesn't change.

SELF-DIAGNOSIS FOR FIRST-ORDER CHANGE: DEFINING POTENTIAL IMPROVEMENT POINTS (PIPS)

In Adizes, we don't speak about "problems," we call the challenges that a person has "PIPs": Potential Improvement Points. If we define something as a problem we may be prematurely finalizing and become close-minded to inputs that we might be wrong. The word PIP was created to keep our mind open: potential improvement point. Anything that can be improved for whatever reason is a PIP. It should be accumulated, deliberated, etc and when finalized it becomes "the problem."

What is a PIP?

*A PIP is your perception of a **controllable** result or process, that is **undesired and/or unexpected**.*

It is something that is within your power to do something about it, in your personal or professional life that is unwanted and/or that you didn't foresee.

Here are some examples of PIPs:

- I am spending too much money.
- I feel stuck in my career.
- I am overweight.
- I am always late.

If you can do something about the above challenges, and it is within your capacity to change the situation, then those are PIPs. If there is nothing you can do about an issue or a situation, it is not a PIP. Here are some examples of non-PIPs:

- The city is not building enough parking places around my office. (You can't change the city's decisions.)
- My friend acts immaturely in her marriage. (You can't change her or take responsibility for her.)
- The elementary school curriculum at my daughter's school is outdated. (You can't change the public education system.)

It is possible, however, to reframe the complaint (and turn it into a PIP), by rephrasing it to be controllable. For example:

- I do not always give myself enough time to park and then get into my office (and I've never looked into using public transportation).
- I have not decided what to do about my immature friend.
- I have not yet decided if I will move my child to a better school.

For a problem to be a PIP it must be controlable. Otherwise, you are just having a self-pity, gripe session over something you can't control.

If a PIP is not controllable and is chronic, get professional help. Do not think that time will heal it. Problems either get better or worse. And to make a situation better you must work on it. Nothing gets better by itself. Period. So you either control it or get help.

SELF-COACHING PROTOCOL FOR FIRST-ORDER CHANGE

What is the PIP I want to solve?............................

My lifecycle stage:..

Is the PIP related to my current lifecycle stage? Yes/No

Is it a normal and expected lifecycle-stage problem? Yes/No

What is the missing PAEI vitamin that, if administered, would solve this problem?..

How can I administer this missing vitamin? (Answer the five imperatives.)

- **What** is it that I need to do? (Define the desired result in measurable terms.)
- **How** am I going to do it? (Specify the exact steps you need to take.)
- **By when** would I like to reach this goal? (Set a realistic timeline.)
- **Who** can support me in doing this? (Think about who can help you and ask them for their help.)
- **Why** is this important to me? Think in terms of values and needs. What need/value are you trying to satisfy.)

Then off you go, to implement your plan.

If you cannot obtain the desired result on or before your specified deadline:

- **By when**: Change the timeline. Perhaps the deadline you set was not realistic. Give yourself more time.
- **Why**: Ask yourself, "How long have I been having this problem? How will I feel if I still have this problem two years from now?" Leverage the pain the thought of not solving this problem causes you, to see if this will prompt you to act.
- **Who**: Get more help. If solving your problem requires assistance. Ask others to give you a hand.

If you still can't make progress, it's time to go deeper. Check to see if you have limiting beliefs that are creating noise and preventing you from getting this problem solved. In other words, it may be that first-order change is not enough, and a second-order change inquiry is needed.

Let's look at some case studies of individuals who used self-coaching to accomplish first-order change.

Case study #1: Joseph, 16 years old

What is the PIP I want to solve? (In this case study there is more than one PIP) Unhappy with pace of progress in bodybuilding and self-image; scattered, can't stick to already successful workout program

My lifecycle stage: Adolescence

Is the PIP related to my current lifecycle stage? Yes

Is it a normal and expected lifecycle-stage problem? Yes

What is the missing PAEI vitamin that, if administered, would solve this problem? (A)

How can I administer this missing vitamin?

- **What** is it that I need to do?
  - I need to diligently persist (P) with my existing program (A).
- **How** am I going to do it?
  - I'll block times in calendar (A) and do it no matter what (P).
  - I'll stop looking for new training programs in the hope of finding one that could provide "even better" results (E).
  - I'll measure my different muscles sizes and track them to make sure progress is being made (A).
- **By when** would I like to reach this goal?
  - Six months
- **Who** can support me in doing this?
  - My cousin is a licensed physiotherapist whom I'll consult regarding the pain I keep feeling in my left shoulder during my workouts. He is also very motivating and support-

ive of my goal.

- **Why** is this important to me?
  - When my body image improves, I feel a boost in my self-esteem and as a teenager this is very important to me.

Case study #2: Abe, 46 years old

What is the PIP I want to solve? Feel obsolete in my career

My lifecycle stage: Middle Age, professionally aging quickly due to technological change in his industry (Web development and graphic design)

Is the PIP related to my current lifecycle stage? Yes

Is it a normal and expected lifecycle-stage problem? Yes

What is the missing PAEI vitamin that, if administered, would solve this problem? (E)

How can I administer this missing vitamin?

- **What** is it that I need to do?
  - I need to improve my professional skills and rekindle my creativity and passion in order to reconvert my career.
- **How** am I going to do it?
  - I'll schedule four blocks of time per week (A) during which I will brainstorm my options (E).
  - I'll google success stories of graphic designers who have reinvented themselves professionally to see if one or more of the niches they moved into suits me.
  - I'll get training in the new areas I discover to obtain miss-

ing skills and competencies (E).

- **By when** would I like to reach this goal?

  › Four months to clarify my direction, then eight months to implement it, for a total of one year to be in a new place

- **Who** can support me in doing this?

  › I'll obtain a loan for continuing-education classes.

- **Why** is this important to me?

  › I am a creative person and want to feel again the passion I once had for my profession.

ADIZES FOR SECOND-ORDER CHANGE

Sometimes life presents you with more complex challenges, which cannot be solved with the relatively simple protocols presented in the previous section. It's one thing to be deciding which college best suits your education needs, but it's quite another when a crisis in your relationship leads to a crisis in your career (and then you discover a crisis in your health). The first can be addressed with first-order change self-coaching. The latter requires second-order change and a more systemic and sophisticated protocol—if you are to get a broader and deeper awareness of the problem and its potential solutions.

In second-order change, growth is often required, and you may see a change in the relative size of each PAEI role in your code.

SELF-DIAGNOSIS FOR SECOND-ORDER CHANGE

The diagnostic process for second-order change is comprised of six main parts:

1. Know yourself

2. Accumulate
3. Spread
4. Illuminate
5. State the problem
6. Get leverage

Diagnosis begins with knowing yourself. All personal growth begins with your own understanding of what makes you tick. Once you have this information you can move on to analyzing and interpreting the data you have gathered—to look for patterns of causality and get a big-picture view of the problem and its root causes. When this is complete, you will be ready to clearly state your problem and set a goal to solve it in clear and measurable terms.

First Stage: Know yourself

To achieve second-order change it is imperative to go deeper and understand yourself better. The first step is to do a quick mapping of yourself:[1] to find your PAEI style and determine your location on the lifecycle curve. It's also often useful to understand where you are in your family lifecycle and in your professional/organizational lifecycle, as these systems continuously interact with each other.[2] As well, find out what values drive and motivate you.

---

1. We recommend a basic education in Adizes tools. As with many other coaching and therapeutic modalities, it's important to get educated in the theory behind the tools. This can be done by reading Part 2 of this book, and (as you progress), aiming to cover all Adizes literature according to your needs (organizational, family, individual). A full list of books, videos, trainings, and other resources is provided at the end of this book.

2. A person may be in one stage in their individual lifecycle, and in another stage in their organizational or family lifecycle. For instance, a start-up Entrepreneur may be going through the struggles of the Infancy stage in her professional lifecycle, while just entering the Adolescence/Turbulence stage in her family lifecycle. This is a key understanding, since at this time her business needs the most support from her family, yet the latter is in turmoil and heavy infighting (which drains energy instead of providing it).

Second Stage: Accumulate

The second step is to collect all of your PIPs. Look at the different parts of your life and do a "brain dump." Make a list of every problem that comes to mind.

Examples of PIPs:

- "Lack of self-rewards"
- "My life is boring."
- "My old car breaks continuously."
- "My old PC at home is not powerful enough for Zoom meetings."
- "The pandemic is limiting my income."
- "I am lonely."

Third Stage: Spread

Once you have a full list of PIPs you can proceed to what we call the "spreading" of the PIPs across an "Attribution Matrix." The Attribution Matrix is a central tool in the Adizes Methodology. Simply put, it is a six-column, boxed-matrix spreadsheet that allows you to assign PIPs into different categories. These categories will allow you to determine:

1. *What is falling apart* for you?
2. *What is the chain of causality?* Problems are interrelated and these interrelationships can be analyzed in a chain of causality (a cause-and-effect explanation of what is behind the symptoms and manifestations of the problems).

The following diagram shows the structure of the Attribution Matrix, as well as an explanation of its components and their functions:

COLUMN 0 EXTERNAL, NON-CONTROLLABLE PIPS	COLUMN 1 PERSONAL	COLUMN 2 STRUCTURE	COLUMN 3 MISSION & PROCESS	COLUMN 4/5 SUBSYSTEMS	COLUMN 6 MANIFESTATIONS
Col. 0 Box 1 Non-controllable	Col. 1 Box 1 Values	Col. 2 Box 1 Time & Energy	Col. 3 Box 1 Mission	Col. 4/5 Box 1 External Relationships	Col. 6 Box 1 Dysfunctional Behavior
	Col. 1 Box 2 Lifecycle	Col. 2 Box 2 Authority	Col. 3 Box 2 Decision-Making	Col. 4/5 Box 2 Operational Functions	Col. 6 Box 2 Change
Col. 0 Box 2 Influenceable				Col. 4/5 Box 3 My Own Emotional Issues	Col. 6 Box 3 Effectiveness
	Col. 1 Box 3 Styles	Col. 2 Box 3 Rewards	Col. 3 Box 3 Corrective Action	Col. 4/5 Box 4 Money Issues	Col. 6 Box 4 Efficiency

What is falling apart in you?

Each column in the matrix represents the things that may be falling apart in you and in your life. The numbers denote the sequence of the columns in the chain of causality.

Systemic Causes:

0. External, noncontrollable PIPs

1. Personal (behavioral)

2. Structure

3. Mission & Process

4/5. Subsystems (symptoms)

6. Manifestations (systemic, and their consequences)

General tips for "attributing" PIPs into the matrix boxes

- We attribute the PIPs to the different boxes in the matrix, by what is, not by what caused what is.
- If we can't precisely pinpoint a PIP, but we know it exists, then we go by how we will solve it.

- If we can't decide on the how, we attribute a PIP by why we believe it is happening.
- If none of the above quite apply, we attribute a PIP by who will solve it.

Column 0: External, noncontrollable PIPs

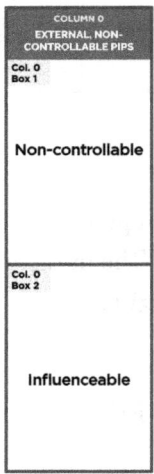

These are the problems that are causing stress in your life, but that you have no control over whatsoever. This column has two boxes:

- **Not controllable**: this box needs to be monitored because the PIPs that reside here might not be controllable now, but they may become controllable in the future.
- **Influenceable**: Meaning, if you can get the parties involved to cooperate, then control of the PIP may be obtained.

Examples of column "0" problems:

"Fear for safety"
"Terrorism"

"Unclean neighborhood"
"Sister is getting divorced"
"Traffic jams when commuting"
"COVID-19 outbreak"
"Bad situation in the country"

Ask yourself: "Is this particular PIP really out of control, or is there a way I can influence it or reframe it to make it controllable?"

"Sister is getting divorced": Is this situation really out of control, or can you do something about it? If there is something you can do to about this situation, then the PIP can be reframed. Perhaps it can be reframed as, "I haven't yet decided how much to put aside from my own finances to help my sister after her divorce." If you cannot help financially, then it is of no use to worry over this inability. It doesn't make you insensitive. You would help financially if it was possible, but if helping your sister financially is not possible then worrying about it will not change this (and it will only drain your energy). The situation is unfortunate, but that is just life. Most likely you **will** help in other ways, such as offering her emotional support.

But if you can do something about a particular PIP, then it doesn't belong in column "0" and it should go somewhere else in the spreadsheet—on one of the columns to the right, where things are controllable, and you can influence and change them.

This brings us to a very important principle of the Attribution Matrix: PIPs are always categorized from left to right, from external and out of our control, to internal and controllable.

As we previously stated, and the Attribution Matrix diagram above illustrates, problems are interrelated and these interrelationships can be analyzed in a chain of causality. The chain is a collection of columns divided into boxes: with the left-side problems typically causing or influencing the problems that appear to the right (plus their

132 SYSTEMIC COACHING

symptoms and manifestations), and the top-level problems typically causing or influencing the problems that appear further down.

CAUSALITY CHAIN					
COLUMN 0 EXTERNAL, NON-CONTROLLABLE PIPS	COLUMN 1 PERSONAL	COLUMN 2 STRUCTURE	COLUMN 3 MISSION & PROCESS	COLUMN 4/5 SUBSYSTEMS	COLUMN 6 MANIFESTATIONS
Col. 0 / Box 1 Non-controllable	Col. 1 / Box 1 Values	Col. 2 / Box 1 Time & Energy	Col. 3 / Box 1 Mission	Col. 4/5 / Box 1 External Relationships	Col. 6 / Box 1 Dysfunctional Behavior
	Col. 1 / Box 2 Lifecycle	Col. 2 / Box 2 Authority	Col. 3 / Box 2 Decision-Making	Col. 4/5 / Box 2 Operational Functions	Col. 6 / Box 2 Change
Col. 0 / Box 2 Influenceable				Col. 4/5 / Box 3 My Own Emotional Issues	Col. 6 / Box 3 Effectiveness
	Col. 1 / Box 3 Styles	Col. 2 / Box 3 Rewards	Col. 3 / Box 3 Corrective Action	Col. 4/5 / Box 4 Money Issues	Col. 6 / Box 4 Efficiency

Column 1: Personal

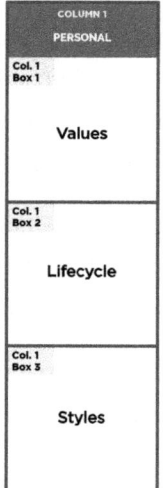

Box 1.1: Values

In this box, you include all those PIPs that relate to your personal values.

Examples of PIPs that go into this box:

"I am obsessed with career progress and money"
"I feel I am not doing enough for other people"
"Order and rules are paramount to me in my life. I love my space to be organized, clean, and properly structured"

We identify a person's values using Don Beck's SDi (Spiral Dynamics) system.[3] This system identifies how humanity's value systems evolved from one paradigm of thinking to the next throughout history. SDi gives a roadmap for understanding our values.

---

3. See *Spiral Dynamics: Mastering Values, Leadership, and Change*, by Don Beck and Christopher Cowan, 1996, 2005, Wiley/Blackwell.

SPIRAL DYNAMICS: WHAT ARE YOUR VALUES?

Spiral Dynamics recognizes the following paradigms—each offering a full "package" of values and a way of thinking, and looking at life, relationships, work, and the world:

1. Beige
2. Purple
3. Red
4. Blue
5. Orange
6. Green
7. Yellow/Turquoise

Let's review each of these paradigms and try to see in which one(s) you can identify in yourself.

Beige

This is a very primary, basic, survivalistic paradigm. It is mostly about doing what you need to do just to stay alive. When you value survival your focus is on safety: how to get water, protection, food, and shelter. From a Maslowian-hierarchy-of-needs perspective, we could say that when you need to struggle for these kinds of things, nothing else can take priority. Psychologically, this is a very instinctual way of living, and there is little awareness of the self.

Who uses this value system? We see it as active in newborn babies and the senile elderly.

Positive characteristics of the Beige paradigm:

- It allows you to access your instincts.
- It connects you to your body intelligence.

Downside of the Beige paradigm (if it becomes the main paradigm guiding your life, or if you overuse it):

- Exclusively biological existence; no place for the psychological
- Automatic, habit-driven existence
- Living "off the land," trying to make it through the day
- Very limited focus—mainly on providing basic human needs
- No awareness of "me" as a distinct entity

Purple

Once people succeed in achieving the Beige level, new needs arise, and a new paradigm is required. This seems to follow the famous Einstein saying: "We cannot solve our problems with the same thinking we used when we created them."

When people organize themselves in clans, families, and tribes, survival becomes easier, and all the effort required to provide basic needs is now liberated for resources that can be used for higher, psychological needs.

Purple attempts to give an answer to the human need to understand reality, to make sense of the world. With Purple, we see the appearance of the first models of reality, which are based mainly on mystical views.

Who uses this value system? It is active among groups such as tribes and sports teams.

Positive characteristics of the Purple paradigm:

- Access to metaphysics
- Emergence of family and group dynamics (instead of my needs and my survival, it's now our needs and our survival)
- Loyalty to family and group
- Ability to connect through imagination, rituals, and tradition; respect for traditions, hymns, and flags
- Downside of the Purple paradigm (if it becomes the main paradigm guiding your life, or if you overuse it):
- Superstitions. Accessing metaphysics is one thing, but automatic attribution of causality in a superstitious way is quite another ("Because I wore my blue shirt, this or that happened").
- Loyalty can deteriorate into overcommitting to a group—to the point that your life belongs to the tribe (example: the kamikaze pilots in World War II).

Red

Purple, at its peak, creates an overemphasis on the group at the expense of the individual. With time, the individual dimension suffers, giving birth to conditions that lead to the next paradigm, Red.

In Red, the individual reclaims power and the willingness to exert independent control over one's own life. A break from the pack therefore occurs. There is a feeling of "we are on our own" and that "life is tough out there," so one needs to reject limits and be strong to survive. Life in the Red paradigm feels like a jungle.

The primary drive is power: to dominate and express oneself in the world without limitations.

Who uses this value system? It is active among warlords, Mafia leaders, conquerors, and rock stars.

Positive characteristics of the Red paradigm:

- Assertiveness
- Resilience in difficult times
- Ability to recover and continue against all odds, not giving up easily
- Using gut instincts to trade and make a living, activation of instincts
- Downside of the Red paradigm (if it becomes the main paradigm guiding your life, or if you overuse it):
- Aggressiveness
- Remorselessly going after what one wants, "like a bulldozer" when needed.
- An animalistic/survivalist view of the human race. "Dog eat dog." "Eat or be eaten."
- Egocentrism

When this is your worldview, you believe that you had better be strong or you may be eaten alive.

According to most developmental psychologists, Red marks the first appearance in human history of organizations and people working in them and for them. Organizations that apply the pure Red spirit dominate the people that work for them in different ways. Because Red is an individualistic paradigm, these organizations are typically founded by a strong individual who reigns with an iron fist over the subordinates. In the extreme, we see slavery and Mafia-type organizations, where "life is a jungle and you better be strong" applies literally.

In less extreme but still illegal forms, you find Red in criminal organizations and the behind the scandals of famous CEOs—accused of harassing and misusing employees and other unconstrained behaviors. In milder, legal forms, you can see Red in today's organizations that battle fiercely in the marketplace: in monopolies, in the hostile takeover of companies, and in the ruthless "Gordon Gekko" style of management (well portrayed by Michael Douglas in the movie Wall Street).

Blue

At its point of saturation, Red causes the need for humanity to create law and order to prevent its own excesses. Humanity's response to Red is the Blue paradigm. Conditions of living become such that they pave the way for and naturally liberate this next system of values. There is a shift from "what I want" to "what the system wants." In other words, Blue appears as response to a societal need to contain individual negative impulses and restore control and power within society.

Who uses this system of values? We see it in religions, bureaucracies, armies, and cultures (such as Singapore).

If you are an order-driven person, you will identify with this value system.

Positive characteristics of the Blue paradigm:

- Brings order and stability
- Creates a code of conduct and ethics
- Enforces principles and laws
- Respects tradition
- Creates predictability and safety
- Seeks efficiency and control

Downside of the Blue paradigm (if it becomes the main paradigm guiding your life, or if you overuse it):

- Rigidity
- "Either/or" thinking (Things are either right or wrong.)
- Linear thinking; conceives phenomena in a linear fashion, as if events always occur on a straight line from A to B
- Looks at life too bureaucratically, emphasis is on control
- May stifle an individual with a generic, one-size-fits-all approach to everything
- Tasks and obligations first, people second
- People must obey the laws, regardless of how they feel about them. Punishment for disobedience
- People must be told what to do and be controlled and monitored in order to obtain results.
- Conditions people to decide based on fear of consequences instead of encouraging true choice
- Keeping the status quo at all costs

Orange

Blue brings order to the world, but too much order and control and you begin to have too big of a push toward conformism and obedience: People are expected to do exactly as they are told, and there is no room for creativity and innovation. Orange appears as a response to that. In Orange, humanity returns to a desire for freedom and progress. And the Orange paradigm does this by once again empowering the individual.

In Orange, people begin to understand that authority may, or may not, be the answer to everything and that individual learning and responsibility for one's own life are also important. Based on this shift, and for almost three hundred years, humanity has witnessed colossal revolutions. Individual empowerment has brought forth the emergence of the researcher: one who is allowed to create inventions and explore the world. In aggregate, this led to the scientific revolution and the birth of the modern sciences. Orange has grown as a global paradigm—to the point of becoming, in recent decades, the dominant worldview in business and politics.

Who uses this value system? Entrepreneurs, the corporate world.

Positive characteristics of the Orange paradigm:

- Empowers the individual and originates the "enterprising self" (away from the compliant stereotype created by Blue bureaucracies)
- Practical, fast paced
- Modernization of society, unprecedented prosperity

- Fosters individuals who take responsibility for their destiny
- Invites possibility: The sky is the limit of what can be achieved if one works hard toward a goal. And for the first time in history, anybody can move up the ladder based on merit. (Blue has a tendency to arbitrarily define who belongs to which social class and to preserve that as the status quo.)

Downside of the Orange paradigm (if it becomes the main paradigm guiding your life, or if you overuse it):

- Denies/casts people's feelings aside in order to be more efficient
- An "end-justifies-the-means" approach that seeks progress and winning at all costs, while ignoring principles and ethics
- Measures success only in terms of status, prestige, and material progress
- To advance and win, unhealthy Orange may uncaringly destroy the environment and nature's ecosystem, unscrupulously overexploit the Earth's resources, coldheartedly dehumanize the work force (forcing people to work as soulless machines and creating generations of workaholics), and dangerously use debt to leverage risky deals for quick profit—all without considering the long-term consequences of his or her own actions. To Orange, the only important thing is "whatever works now and allows me to climb." Fostering consumerism is a way of life (distorting values and placing material success above all). This utter lack of humanity—putting

material progress before human value—generates moral crises and is too strong against the Blue paradigm. As a result Blue morals and integrity are lost.

Green

Reaching its peak in America over the last decades, the Orange paradigm began to cause a series of disasters that—as a reaction to its destruction—paved the way for the appearance of the Green paradigm. Increasingly, the media began to report (as they do to this day) one Orange scandal after another: corporate greed, shady deals, financial meltdowns, ecological damage. All were portraits of unhealthy Orange in action, unstoppable in its relentless pursuit of "more."

With the awakening of Green, it has been realized that the economic bottom line cannot be the only objective and can no longer be the sole compass that guides humanity.

Who uses this paradigm? If you are driven by human connection and are socially conscious, you identify with the Green paradigm.

Positive characteristics of the Green paradigm:

- Pluralism, equality, inclusiveness
- Proactivity for human rights and community building
- People are not "machines" and cannot be treated as such in their personal and professional lives.
- Life cannot be a rat race; it's important to stop and think about the meaning of it all.
- Company culture is important: a company is a big family, with a value-based mission statement, where every

person should be made to feel that he or she belongs. Green companies aim to care about the individual, the community, and the world.

- Teamwork is important. Employees should be listened to empathetically, and they should be nurtured, developed, and supported.
- It's essential that everyone's voice is heard and decisions are made by consensus.
- The environment should be protected and cared for.
- Downside of the Green paradigm (if it becomes the main paradigm guiding your life, or if you overuse it):
- In spite of its good intentions, Green can take a combative stance and equate corporations and everything Orange with "evil."
- Coming on too strong against people who don't align with Green principles
- Too extreme a tendency to abolish structures and rules. Green can take an extremely combative position, not only against Orange, but also against Blue. This leaves a void of rules that can be extremely problematic. Permissiveness becomes a Green side effect, not only in the corporate world but in other areas as well (such as parenting and education).
- Relativism and "horizontalization": Everything is equally important. When the absolutes are abolished, everything is true in the same measure. No one truth can be possible, only interpretations of truth.

Yellow and Turquoise ("Second-Tier Paradigms")

Green is an important paradigm in the evolution of consciousness because it comes to correct the grave distortions produced by Blue and Orange, but it does so in a way that still reflects a war between paradigms and value systems. Because of this, at a certain level, Green becomes better at diffusing Blue and Orange excesses than at proposing effective alternatives that can be put into practice.

The First "Tier" of paradigms consists of Beige, Purple, Red, Blue, Orange, and Green levels. In the First Tier, each meme, or paradigm color, is against another meme. When Blue appears, it does so in reaction to the chaos that Red creates. When Orange appears, it is a reaction to Blue's compulsion for control. And when Green appears, it does so as a reaction to Orange, Blue, and Red excesses.

The word reaction is key here, because the First Tier is characterized by reactivity. And reactivity is ego based; as such, it causes people to react against each other, and to enter into wars against each other.

Some examples of how these intermeme fights happen include:

- "I am an environmentalist and I hate corporations. They are all evil and greedy." (Unhealthy Green indiscriminately against Orange)
- "I am bottom-line oriented. Don't be a crybaby. I want people who produce. I can't empathize and be a therapist for my employees!" (Unhealthy Orange and Red indiscriminately against Green)

- "People cannot be trusted. They need to be told what to do and supervised. Otherwise nothing gets done." (Unhealthy Blue indiscriminately against Green)

The Yellow and Turquoise paradigms are the first paradigms to come along with the ability to unite all memes and stop the wars between them. It's a shift to a different order, a major leap in awareness.

In the Second Tier …

We see the value and contribution of all previous memes and seek to integrate them.

- We step away from identifying with solely one meme and from being against all other memes.
- We become "meme appreciators," and accept that all memes are necessary, at healthy doses, and for different purposes.
- We move from "either/or" thinking to "and" thinking, with the ability to integrate differing perspectives and embrace paradox.

The Second Tier is a leap to a different dimension of consciousness, because the fragmentation caused by ego is no longer there, (thus allowing love to truly happen). First Tier memes are division paradigms: they divide people, they put people in an "us against them" egoic mentality.

The Second-Tier values are based on the notion that the whole of humanity is connected at a deeply spiritual level and there is an underlying oneness to all things.

146   SYSTEMIC COACHING

Box 1.2: Lifecycle

These are the PIPs that derive from where you are on the lifecycle curve.

Examples of PIPs that go into this box:

"I am having a midlife crisis."
"I am already thinking like an old person even though my body still looks fine."
"My kids left home, and I am not sure how to make a transition into this new stage in life."

Box 1.3: Styles

These are the PIPs that derive from your PAEI style.[4]

Examples of PIPs that go into this box:

"I am easily distracted by the new ideas and projects in my mind."

"I can't stand still. I'm always in constant motion."

Column 2: Structure

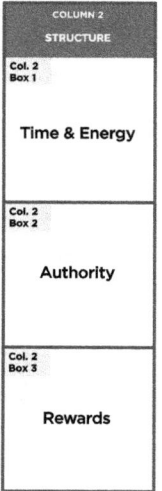

4.   To learn more about your own personal style, see Part 2/Chapter 2: "PAEI as a code for personality style."

Box 2.1: Time and Energy

Here we attribute PIPs that deal with how you structure your time and energy to take care of the different areas of your life.

Examples of PIPs that go into this box:

"In our family, it is not clear how we should organize our mother's care."
"I am overwhelmed at work because I am responsible for the results of the whole HR department."

Box 2.2: Authority

Here we attribute PIPs that deal with issues pertaining to authority.

Examples of PIPs that go into this box:

"My wife/husband makes all the decisions. I feel disempowered."
"I have no control over my expenses."
"Our family budget is not honored."
"My decisions are perceived only as recommendations. I feel ignored."

Box 2.3: Rewards

Here we attribute PIPs that deal with issues of rewarding/punishing oneself.

What makes you feel rewarded? Many get the feeling of being rewarded outside of home. They find rewards in their town, in their work. Others don't feel professionally happy, and they may feel rewarded only in their friendships. It's normal to be drawn to where we feel most appreciated.

Examples of PIPs that go into this box:

"I feel guilty when I take some time off."
"I diet during the week, but on Sundays I have a "cheat day" and eat myself sick, to the point of not being able to work the next day."

Column 3: Mission & Process

Box 3.1: Mission

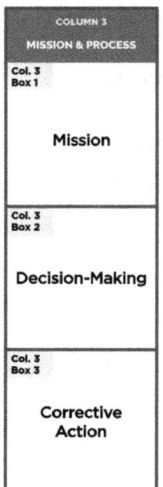

Here you attribute PIPs that deal with how you want your life to be.

Example of a PIPs that goes into this box:

"I don't have a long-term purpose and plan."

Box 3.2: Decision-Making

Decision-making involves listening to the four voices in your head (P, A, E, and I) and discerning what to do regarding a particular situation. You are "communicating with yourself" and deciding which role would be appropriate in each situation. When this internal process gets broken, you'll have PIPs related to decision-making.

Examples of PIPs that go into this box:

"Instead of weighing my options, I finalize decisions on important matters impulsively."

Box 3.3: Corrective Action

Here we attribute PIPs that deal with how you learn from past mistakes and to what degree corrective measures are being taken.

Examples of PIPs that go into this box:

"I am not learning from my mistakes; I constantly fall back into my negative past behaviors."
"This is the third time this year that I have gotten a ticket because I parked in the wrong place in my neighborhood."

Column 4/5: Subsystems

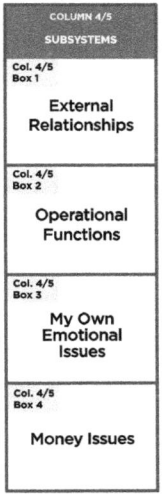

Box 4.1: External Relationships

Who is "your client" in life? Whom should you take care of? Children? Aging parents? Your partner? Some people feel a responsibility toward the community they live in or belong to. They volunteer with their synagogue, their church, or the homeless.

Thus, in this box we attribute those PIPs that pertain to "not doing a good enough job" for those "clients."

Examples of PIPs that fall into this subsystem:

"I am constantly finding new reasons to avoid volunteering at my church."
"I am very, very busy and hardly see my children."

Box 4.2: Operational functions

This subsystem includes all of the physical and operational activities required to run your life, as well as the routines that keep you organized, productive, well-maintained, and functional.

Examples of PIPs that fall into this subsystem:

"I live alone. When I come home from work, I am overwhelmed by household chores, but I can't pay for help."
"My car lights are broken, and I never have time to take it to the garage."

Box 4.3: My own emotional issues

This subsystem includes all the problems that you may have in developing self-trust and self-respect, or that are interfering and preventing you from growing.

Examples of PIPs that fall into this subsystem:
"I haven't had any career boosts in a long time."
"I am not growing as a person."

Box 4.4: Money issues

This subsystem deals with the handling of financial resources.

Examples of PIPs that fall into this subsystem:

"I don't have any kind of budget."
"I feel afraid every time my credit card statement arrives."

Column 6: Manifestations

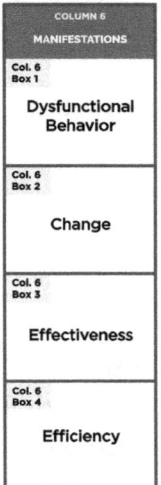

Columns 0–3 identified the causes that explain our situation, and column 4/5 reflected the symptoms. Column 6 describes the consequences, or manifestations, those problems are triggering.

Many PIPs arise as long-term consequences of past bad mistakes, sooner or later these consequences and manifestations surface. These consequences are expressed in PAEI terms, with one box corresponding to each of the four PAEI roles.

Box 6.1: Dysfunctional Behavior

Here we attribute PIPs that deal with manifestations you are having in the (I) realm.

Examples of PIPs that go into this box:

"I am depressed."
"I get angry quite often at work."

Box 6.2: Change

Here we attribute PIPs that deal with manifestations you are having in the (E) realm.

Examples of PIPs that go into this box:

"My life is boring."
"Nothing is new."

Box 6.3: Effectiveness

Here we attribute PIPs that deal with the manifestations you are having in the (P) realm. In other words, those PIPs that deal with consequences caused by a lack of effectiveness, such as negativity or feeling a lack of achievement.

Examples of PIPs that go into this box:

"I have not finished my degree."
"I have not cleaned my house for weeks."
"I do not see my parents often enough."
"I am not doing well in my job."

Box 6.4: Efficiency

Here we attribute PIPs that deal with the manifestations you are having in the (A) realm. In other words, those PIPs that deal with consequences caused by a lack of efficiency, such as a prolonged waste of resources.

Examples of PIPs that go into this box:

"I am financially broke"
"My credit-card debt will take so long to be repaid."

We have now spread our PIPs out on the Attribution Matrix, which was the third diagnostic stage for second-order change. Now, let's move on to the remaining stages.

Fourth and Fifth Stages: Illuminate and state the problem

Once all of your PIPs have been assigned to their respective boxes, we move on to the spreadsheet illumination stage. Here, we try to see how everything fits together. As previously stated, the root problems in the left-side columns (0–3) are causing the symptoms and manifestations that we see in the columns to the right (4–6).

The following pages illustrate the process of attribution through a case study ("Attribution Matrix Case Study: Bob") that follows the diagnostic process from the accumulation of PIPs through to the complete statement of the problem.

The statement of the problem officially finalizes the diagnosis stage. When the diagnosis has been determined, we can then move into what to do about it (i.e., how to solve the problem). You will see as you analyze the diagnostic process that a problem is not just one PIP or a series of PIPs, it is how they are interrelated. Often, a person will try to solve just one PIP. This is a common mistake. The key is to break the "PIP chain." This diagnostic approach allows us to see the big picture of the problem, almost like taking an aerial snapshot of the situation.

Sixth (and final) Stage: Get leverage

Problems cause pain and drain your energy. The more pain that is caused and the more energy that is drained, the higher the opportunity to use this pain as fuel to find a solution. When you are totally fed up with a problem, you are ready to change. In coaching, leveraging is the technique of asking questions to connect a coachee with accumulated pain caused by PIPs. . In Adizes Coaching you get leverage through "Oh, sh**" questions. As you finalize the diagnosis stage, the leveraging technique prompts you to find a solution and motivates you to implement it.

As you look at the statement of Bob's problem and the accumulation of his PIPs, consider how Bob may have reacted when we asked these questions:

1. How many of these PIPs did you have last year?
2. How many of these PIPs did you have two years ago?
3. Now for the "Oh, sh**" question: **How many of the PIPs that you have had for two years or more will you still have next year?**

Bob's answer will most likely be: Many.

Leverage question: *If you had a magic pill that ensured you would act in an integrated fashion, with the four voices in your head in harmony (in other words: if you didn't have any confusion regarding what to do, how to do it, when to do it, with whom to do it, and why you should do it),[5] and you were acting from your best self, with total self-trust and self-respect, how many of these PIPs would be solved?*

By definition—because Bob's coach asked him to accumulate only the PIPs that are controllable (i.e., to be solved by Bob)—the answer should be: ALL OF THEM.

Now what is the problem itself? The problem is not what Bob has written here, what Bob has written is a manifestation of his problem. The problem is that Bob is not "together." He is disintegrating or disintegrated. The voices in his head cannot come to an agreement (about what, how, by when, and who should do it) and the self-interest is not strong enough to activate Bob to do something about his situation.

---

5. See Part 2, "Foundational Tool #2, How we make decisions: the four voices in our head," for
a more in-depth discussion on healthy decision-making and the imperatives required to make a
complete decision.

Attribution matrix case study: BOB

Bob is 39 years old, and he is going through a personal crisis. This is how he filled out the self-coaching attribution matrix.

Accumulation of PIPs:

- "I don't have a long-term mission and my life feels purposeless."
- "I work too much, 16 hours a day."
- "I am obsessed with achievement."
- "I overeat and have poor health habits."
- "I am stressed."
- "I am 39 years old and cannot commit to my girlfriend."
- "My finances are in trouble."
- "My doctor has warned that I am at high risk for a heart attack."
- "My house is always a mess."
- "My daughter from my first marriage doesn't speak to me."
- "Life feels boring and miserable."

Spreading:

Bob then proceeded to assign the PIPs to boxes in the Attribution Matrix, as follows:

PIP	Box
"I don't have a long-term mission and my life feels purposeless."	3.1 Mission

PIP	Box
"I work too much, sixteen hours a day."	1.3 Style
"I am obsessed with achievement."	1.1 Values
"I overeat and have poor health habits."	6.1 Dysfunctional Behavior
"I am stressed".	6.3 Effectiveness
"I am 39 years old and cannot commit to my girlfriend."	4.1 External Relationships
"My finances are in trouble."	4.4 Money Issues
"My doctor has warned that I am at high risk for a heart attack."	6.3 Effectiveness
"My house is always a mess."	4.2 Operational Functions
"My daughter from my first marriage doesn't speak to me."	4.1 External Relationships
"Life feels boring and miserable."	6.2 Change

Bob's Attribution Matrix looked like this:

Illumination and statement of the problem

Bob then proceeded to find patterns (remember, going from left to right in the chain of causality). This was his illumination:

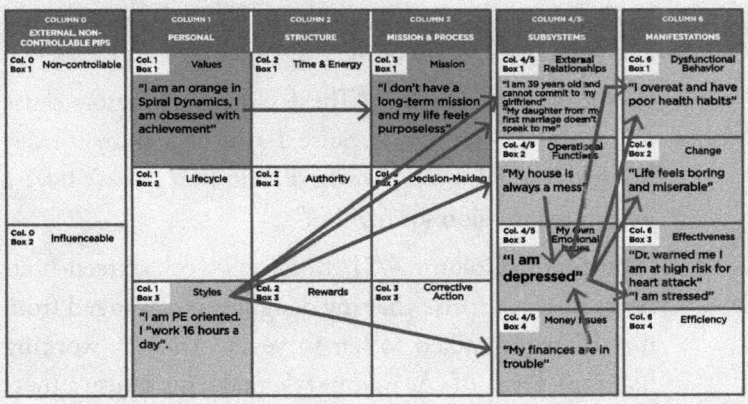

Two main patterns surfaced immediately. The first (marked in dark grey) originated from his extreme (PE) style, with very low (A) which caused problems in several of his subsystems: with his daughter and current girlfriend; and with the way he handles his home and his finances. All of this seemed to be causing overeating and poor health habits, which in turn also worsened his stress and put him at risk of a heart attack.

The second pattern (marked in light grey) was more existential in nature and exposed a crisis value: as an extreme orange in Spiral Dynamics, he was obsessed with achievements and material success (to the detriment of everything else in his life), leaving him empty and without a sense of mission and purpose.

The patterns also seemed to be interconnected, with light blue—obsession with achievement—fueling an unhealthy PE working style.

The statement of the problem then, read like this:

- [Pointing to Column 1] "My values make me very driven. I am orange in Spiral Dynamics. That makes me work too much. And my style, which is lacking in (A) and (I), causes me to be very disorganized and messy."
- [Pointing to Column 3] "These Column 1 factors cause me an inner conflict, because I run like crazy all day but feel like I'm going nowhere, and that I don't have a long-term mission for my life."
- [Pointing to Column 4/5] "Because I work sixteen-hour days, it's no surprise that my daughter is estranged from me. I haven't talked to her in years. And my working habits and lack of (A) in my style make my house a mess and also cause me to lack control in my budget. As a result, my finances are in trouble. My girlfriend is upset with me for not committing to her; my daughter is angry at me for not communicating with her; a messy house and financial difficulties make me depressed and cause me to …"

[Pointing to Column 6] eat excessively and I feel life is miserable."

COACHING AND PROBLEM-SOLVING FOR SECOND-ORDER CHANGE

Relieve, Arrest, or Solve?

Once the diagnosis has been finalized, we proceed to the problem-solving stage. Our goal is to solve the PIPs. The question that arises is, what should be addressed first? Which PIP should we pick?

At this point, a powerful principle comes into play that states: While the causality chain goes from left to right—with the less-controllable PIPs in the left-side columns explaining the PIPs, symptoms, and manifestations in the right-side columns—the solution chain goes in reverse. As the old saying goes, "The fish stinks from the head but you clean it from the tail."

To initiate a solution, begin with the columns on the far right: column 4/5 and column 6.

Why? Because in the short-term, it's easier to zero in on and relieve symptoms and arrest manifestations than to immediately solve the less controllable root causes.

For example: A person may have very strong (E) and (P) roles, but be very weak in (A). These personality characteristics go into column 1. This individual is very driven, but due to a lack of order is not being able to establish good health routines or practice proper self-care. These characteristics may be causing the PIPs in column 6, such as "poor health habits." In the short term, it may be easier to work on getting the person to the gym and making some adjustments to their diet than to work on enriching the personality so it can have more (A). Enrichment of the (A) style can be done, but it will take more time. For now, it might be more productive to arrest, or STOP, issues on the surface through working on the PIPs in columns 4/5 and 6. (A) will begin to develop as the PIPs come under control.

The benefit of this relieve-arrest approach is that it replaces inertia with momentum, and the self-coaching begins to build hope, trust, and faith. Energy builds upon itself, and we gain time, as momentum accelerates. This puts us in a much better position to solve deeper issues later (i.e., the PIPs in columns 3, 2, and 1).

Notice how we've just mentioned three steps for our Adizes Coaching work:

1. Arresting
2. Relieving
3. Solving

There are several additional steps, which will be explained in greater detail in the section below:

1. Releasing
2. Finding a solution with the 4 PAEI imperatives
3. Implementing

Let's now take a look at the Attribution Matrix with the Causality Chain and the Solution Chain in place, and see how these strategies fit into the picture:

CAUSALITY CHAIN →					
COLUMN 0 EXTERNAL, NON-CONTROLLABLE PIPS	COLUMN 1 PERSONAL	COLUMN 2 STRUCTURE	COLUMN 3 MISSION & PROCESS	COLUMN 4/5 SUBSYSTEMS	COLUMN 6 MANIFESTATIONS
Col. 0 Box 1 Non-controllable	Col. 1 Box 1 Values	Col. 2 Box 1 Time & Energy	Col. 3 Box 1 Mission	Col. 4/5 Box 1 External Relationships	Col. 6 Box 1 Dysfunctional Behavior
	Col. 1 Box 2 Lifecycle	Col. 2 Box 2 Authority	Col. 3 Box 2 Decision-Making	Col. 4/5 Box 2 Operational Functions	Col. 6 Box 2 Change
Col. 0 Box 2 Influenceable				Col. 4/5 Box 3 My Own Emotional Issues	Col. 6 Box 3 Effectiveness
	Col. 1 Box 3 Styles	Col. 2 Box 3 Rewards	Col. 3 Box 3 Corrective Action	Col. 4/5 Box 4 Money Issues	Col. 6 Box 4 Efficiency
MONITOR	RELEASE	SOLVE		RELIEVE	ARREST

← SOLUTION CHAIN

HOW TO MANAGE THE SOLUTION CHAIN

Once you have all of your PIPs laid out in the Attribution Matrix, and a clear statement of your problem has emerged, what should you do next? Where should you start? Which PIPs should be addressed first?

STEP 1: ARRESTING THE MANIFESTATIONS IN COLUMN 6

The best first step is to arrest the manifestations in column 6, which means doing something to stop the deterioration they are causing. You cannot directly solve the PIPs in column 6 because they are manifestations of all the PIPs in the columns to the left of them. The PIPs in column 6 will be solved once the PIPs in the other columns are treated and the problem as a whole is solved, but for now you will arrest them to stop the deterioration they are causing.

In column 6, let's pick the PIP, "Poor Health Habits" (under "6.1: Dysfunctional Behavior").

What needs to be done?

Once a PIP is picked, we ask ourselves: How do we arrest it? What needs to be done to stop this PIP in its tracks? How can we stop the deterioration? Give yourself a deadline by which to apply an implementation plan. Your plan must answer to all five imperatives:

- Why does this need to be done?
- What is to be done?
- How will this be done?
- By when does this needs to be done?
- Who will support me as I implement this plan? You will find that you can arrest some PIPs or patterns by yourself, but

others may need outside collaboration and support. Often, you may realize that you need help from others in order to successfully arrest your problem, because you alone might not have the right, the authority, or the will power to implement certain types of changes.

Choosing a PIP from column 6:

When selecting which PIP to arrest, consider the costs involved. Will arresting this PIP cost you some money? Or energy you might not have? Or time? Then consider the benefits of arresting one PIP or another. Which benefits are higher, or of more importance to you, or seem more immediately attainable? Choose a PIP with value that is higher than the cost. If you must choose a PIP with a higher cost (and this is somehow within your financial ability) just learn to live with it for the time being.

STEP 2: WORK ON RELIEVING THE PIPS IN COLUMN 4/5

Now look at the PIPs in column 4/5, to the left of column 6. Start with "4.1: External Relationships." Again, calculate the cost vs. value ratio.

For each PIP, ask yourself the question: "From whom will I need help to deal with this PIP?" Yet again, perform a cost vs. value analysis. Work through each box one by one until you have reviewed all of the PIPs in all of the boxes in column 4/5.

You have now worked through columns 6 and 4/5, but did you solve the PIPs in those columns?

The answer is "no," because you have not yet addressed the causes of the PIPs in columns 1, 2, and 3.

I believe that often we should wait to address columns 1–3 until we gain confidence from handling the PIPs in columns 4/5 and 6. We need to gain self-confidence, and moreover, we need time. Time is limited. Energy is limited. If we attack our big problems first, as if they are weights at the gym, we risk "getting a hernia." Slow down and build your muscles first. Start with the low hanging fruit, the lighter weights. Prove to yourself that you are capable of taking control of your life. Self-coaching requires momentum, and that's what you are doing while working on columns 6 and 4/5. You are building momentum.

STEP 3: WORK ON SOLVING THE PIPS IN COLUMNS 2 AND 3

As you advance to columns 2 and 3 you will find that you have to go back and forth between them. Start with identifying your "Mission." What is your purpose? What do you want? If your problem is your marriage, what's your vision? Do you envision a traditional marriage for yourself, or perhaps an open marriage? In your vision, what comes first, your career or your family? Your fame or your quality of life? Based on that vision, how should you organize your time?

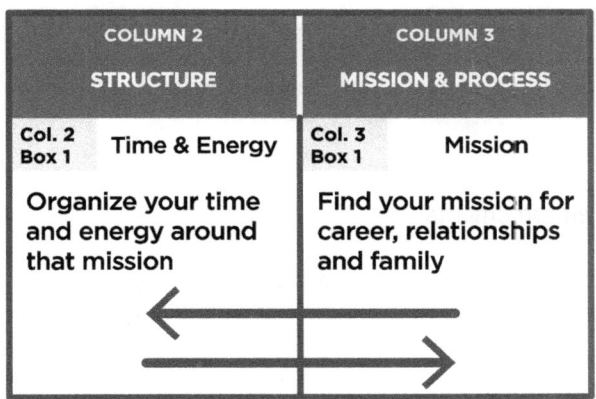

Next move to box 3.2, "Decision-Making," to make sure you are applying your decisions correctly.

Proceed to box 3.3, "Corrective Action." Here you have PIPs for situations that are controllable, that you already know are not right, and yet you are not doing anything about them (such as diet, exercise, spending time with family).

Next, move to box 2.2, "Authority." Who is in charge of your life? Are you really taking responsibility for and owning your problems? Or do you blame your childhood, your parents, your spouse, or your boss? Here, you need to reframe the PIP, until solving it depends only on you.

For example: "My spouse is not helping me with my diet." can be reframed as, "Poor adherence to my diet program." Now you own the problem.

Anytime a PIP is disempowering you, it goes into this box, and you will need to reframe it. Ask yourself: "What can I do that doesn't depend on others? What is it that I am not doing myself?"

Now let's take a look at box 2.3, "Rewards."

Notice how sometimes you need to change the reward system in order to change your behavior, which will then solve your PIPs.

How to use box 2.3 to reinforce behavior that will solve PIPs.

You can reinforce a particular behavior with extrinsic or intrinsic rewards.

Extrinsic reinforcements

There are two types of extrinsic rewards: monetary and nonmonetary.

Monetary

The task you are avoiding provides no personal satisfaction, but money can prompt you to do it.

Example: I very much dislike cleaning and organizing my home, but I'll take $100 and spend it if I get my house organized, to compensate myself for the effort.

Nonmonetary

Here the task is not rewarding, but you feel reinforced by how impressed people are when you do it.

Example: "I don't like doing the dishes. But my spouse is very impressed when I do them, and she holds me in a higher esteem. So I do them even when I'm tired, because I get this reward. She tells everyone how much I help at home, and I love the feeling this gives me."

Intrinsic reinforcements

Intrinsic reinforcements are just the opposite. Performing the task itself provides the reinforcement and external validation is not necessary.

There are four types of intrinsic reinforcements: intrinsic task reward, intrinsic potency reward, intrinsic reinforcement from affiliation, and sense of mission.

Intrinsic task reward

Just having the opportunity to do your job is a reward in itself. For instance, I love to lecture and consult. I can fly all night long and then immediately go to work without feeling tired. I just love lecturing. If I'm asked to do accounting, to balance numbers, you might as well shoot me. So this kind of intrinsic reinforcement depends heavily on my personal preferences. When you do what you like to do, you're inspired; you gain energy instead of expending it. On the other hand, when you do something you hate, you feel sapped of energy. So the task itself is a motivator: I love what I do, and to reward me, just let me do it. An example of an intrinsic task reward is an artist and his art. He may never earn a living from art but take it away from him and see what happens. His heart will be heavy, and he will feel a sense of being punished.

Intrinsic potency reward

When you exercise your power over other people, you feel rewarded. In other words, even if you do not like the task, the fact that you can do it and control the people involved is a source of reinforcement. It makes you feel potent. One example is the bureaucrat: The job is unrewarding and boring. The mission is elusive. There is no potency. There is no power. There is no authority, but they have the power to make you fill out a form again and again, and stand in a line.

Intrinsic reinforcement from affiliation

Each time that people affiliate, and establish friendships and close relationships, they feel a sense of reward. This feeling reinforces their behavior. Social workers and mental health therapists fit into this category. They get a feeling of self-worth from helping people.

Sense of mission

The fulfillment of a mission in which one wholeheartedly believes. An extreme example would be the missionaries who traveled to Africa to convert indigenous peoples to Christianity. They had no power. The task was even dangerous. But they did it because they were fulfilled by their mission.

STEP 4: RELEASING COLUMN 1

The PIPs in column 1 cannot be dealt with directly. Whether value-related PIPs ("I am a blue in Spiral Dynamics and live in an overly conservative way."), lifecycle-related PIPs ("My family is in the Go-Go Stage and our life is a mess."), or style-related PIPs ("I am mainly (EI) and can't get anything done."), you can talk and philosophize about each of them—but it won't make any difference. You need to deal with all of the PIPs from column 6 through column 2 in order to improve the PIPs in column 1.

For example:

Imagine you are a (PA)-oriented person, and people accuse you of being autocratic, of being a control freak that rules with an iron fist and cannot listen well to others. You cannot go to box 1.3, "Styles," and attempt to directly deal with your (PA) style. Rather, you must take all of the PIPs from column 6 and every PIP all the way to the left through column 2, and deal with those in a participative way. In other words, you need to practice not being autocratic, and the PIPs in columns 6–2 will provide you with the platform you need to accomplish this.

> It's in the doing that we change. Not in talking or thinking or complaining.

Coaching for different stages of the lifecycle

The lifecycle box is in column 1, and as such, its PIPs cannot be dealt with directly. You need to work on the PIPs from column 6 to column 1 in a way that will solve your lifecycle-related PIPs.

Looking at the big picture, on the left side of the curve, during the growing stages, the main role that needs to be developed is (A). You must work steadily to develop and increase your sense of self-control (A) so you can get to Prime. And on the right side of the curve, during the aging stages, what needs to be developed is mainly (E). You must steadily obtain and retain your flexibility so as to rejuvenate and remain in (or return to) Prime for as long as possible.[6]

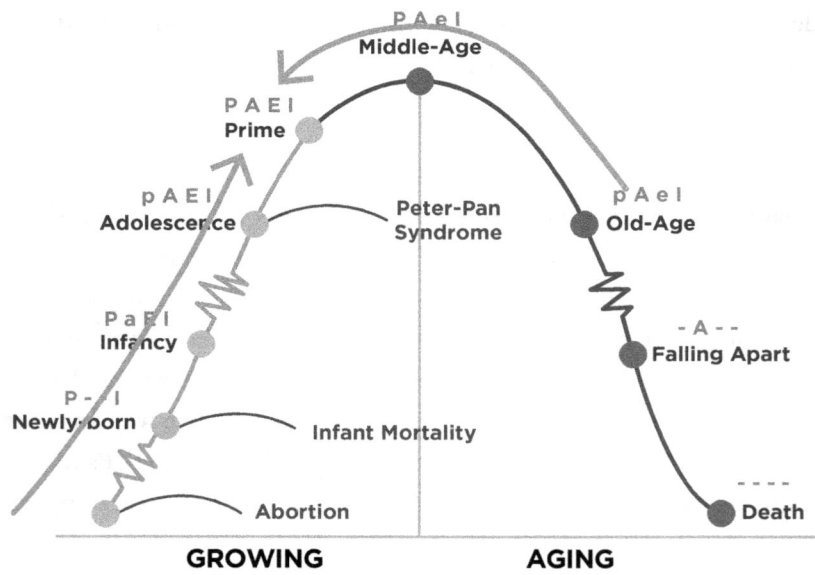

6. Remember, though, that all PAEI roles are needed, and that this only expresses the most important tension along the curve, re: the battle between (E) and (A). It's then key to notice that the recovery strategies along the curve are typically more complex and involve all four roles. Notice for instance, how in the same way that an organization that has become very bureaucratic needs to recover its (E) by first shifting into (P), the same is true for an individual who's already too deep into the Falling Apart stage. In order to rejuvenate themselves via the (E) role, they must first install (P): so their stagnation gets shaken and they start moving. Once that sequence is triggered, it is possible to install (E) and begin the return trip backwards, stage by stage, toward Prime.

But whether in the growing or the aging stages, the missing roles need to be developed through work on columns 6 through 2 of the Matrix, in a way that treats the lifecycle problem.

For instance, if you are in the Old-Age stage, a normal lifecycle PIP to have is the gradual loss of purpose (as children leave home and there is a transition to an empty nest) and the sense of boredom that kicks in.

The main role that needs to be developed, then, is (E). But this PIP resides in column 1, and therefore cannot be dealt with directly. Here is an example:

Case study: Amanda, 53 years old

Amanda's PIPs:

"I can't sleep at night because I get lost on the internet."
"I am depressed."
"My whole schedule has become chaotic and unpredictable."
"I wake up in the morning and have no plans."
"Since my kids left home, I am lost."
"I am continuously fighting with my spouse."
"I am spending way too much money to distract myself."

Spreading the PIPs out in the Attribution Matrix allows for a lifecycle-related pattern to emerge:

Amanda

	COLUMN 0 EXTERNAL, NON-CONTROLLABLE PIPS	COLUMN 1 PERSONAL	COLUMN 2 STRUCTURE	COLUMN 3 MISSION & PROCESS	COLUMN 4/5 SUBSYSTEMS	COLUMN 6 MANIFESTATIONS
Box 1	Col. 0 Non-controllable	Col. 1 Values	Col. 2 Time & Energy "My whole schedule became chaotic and unpredictable"	Col. 3 Mission "I wake up in the morning and have no plans"	Col. 4/5 External Relationships "I am continuously fighting with my spouse"	Col. 6 Dysfunctional Behavior "I can't sleep at night, lost in the Internet"
Box 2	Col. 0 Influenceable	Col. 1 Lifecycle "Since my kids left home I am lost"	Col. 2 Authority	Col. 3 Decision-Making	Col. 4/5 Operational Functions	Col. 6 Change
Box 3		Col. 1 Styles	Col. 2 Rewards	Col. 3 Corrective Action	Col. 4/5 My Own Emotional Issues "I am depressed"	Col. 6 Effectiveness
Box 4					Col. 4/5 Money Issues "I am spending way too much money to distract myself"	Col. 6 Efficiency

Based on the Attribution Matrix, the statement of Amanda's problem could read like this:

"Since my kids left home (lifecycle PIP: box 1.2), my schedule has become unpredictable and chaotic. I no longer wake up with a plan for the day. I am depressed. To distract myself I shop and spend more money than I should. This causes fights with my spouse. After those fights, I end up browsing the Internet for hours, which causes me to lose sleep."

The main vitamin needed is (E). The (E) vitamin needs to be implemented through a reformulation of Amanda's personal mission. Amanda's sense of her mission was deeply tied to being a mom, and now that sense is missing from her life.

The lifecycle PIP (box 1.2), "Since my kids left home …" is underneath Amanda's other PIPs. The main vitamin that is needed is (E), but remember that column 1 PIPs cannot be solved directly.

A new (E) mission is needed in order to pull Amanda toward contributing to something and having a sense of meaning. This would be the main objective of Amanda's coaching: to recover her lost sense of purpose. As the PIPs in columns 6 and 4/5 are arrested and relieved, and Amanda's time and energy increase, her personal schedule (box 2.1) will be adjusted to reflect an investment of time on mission-oriented activities. This will allow to her to alleviate all symptoms and deal appropriately with her lifecycle challenge.

STEP 5: FINDING A SOLUTION WITH THE FOUR PAEI IMPERATIVES

When you want to arrest or solve a PIP, you need to decide on a course of action. In addition, you want to settle on a course of action that will get implemented—not one that will be chosen but nothing happens.

How can you ensure that the decision you make will be implemented in full? To start, you need to ask four questions:

- **What** is my decision?
- **How** is it going to be implemented?
- **By when** do I want it to be implemented?
- **Who** will implement it and who can support me?

Let's say, for instance, that you want to start working out. Here is an example of the four imperatives:

- **What is my decision?**
  - To work out.
- **How is it going to be implemented?**
  - With a dual strategy: two fifteen-minute home workouts

per week, plus two thirty-minute gym workouts per week.

- **By when do I want it to be implemented?**

  › Now.[7]

- **Who will implement it?**

  › I will.

Here is another example. If you pick the task "Eating healthily," then the four imperatives might look like this:

- **What is my decision?**

  › To eat healthily.

- **How is it going to be implemented?**

  › At home and at work, creating a full and complete diet plan for the whole week and taking my own meals to the office.

- **By when do I want it to be implemented?**

  › Now.

- **Who will implement it and who will support me?**

  › I will implement it, with the cooperation of my family.

Now, notice how in this particular example the who imperative depends on the support of other family members. It cannot be done by you alone. Why? Because when you are dieting, you'll want to remove all of the junk food from the house, or at least from your sight, and you'll also need healthy meals. So if the kids are leaving packages of cookies on the kitchen counter, or in the living room, it's going to be hard for you to stick to your diet. You will need your children's

---

7. If you don't start **now**, it will never happen. It's the "manana" syndrome. Remember the famous bar sign on the wall, "free drinks tomorrow", and how they never served a drink.

cooperation. Also, imagine that you are a bad cook, and you will need your spouse's help to prepare your weekly meals. In this case, you will need your children's and your spouse's cooperation. See the point? Sometimes you will be able to implement a solution just by yourself, and other times, as shown here, you will need cooperation those around you. Which brings us, in the next section, to the concept of CAPI.

STEP 6: IMPLEMENTING

You now have the **statement of your problem** and the **solution**. Next, you need create an implementation plan, and that might be the most difficult part. It is not easy to diagnose a problem, and it's a bit more difficult to find a solution, but the real difficulty is that now you have to do it. You need to apply the solution, and this is where many people fail. They know what the problem is, and they know what the solution is, but they do not have the willpower to do much about it. There is an inner struggle. It's as if an internal part of us doesn't want to cooperate.

A lack of cooperation can also come from external sources. As we have said, you can solve some problems by yourself. You do not need help to go to the bathroom unless you are a baby, you are very old, or you are disabled. But to start a new business, to move to a new home, to change jobs, to have children, you need the cooperation at least of your spouse if not of other people.

When this is the case, what happens if the person you need refuses to cooperate? You won't be able to effectively follow through on the decision you have made.

Let's take a more in-depth look at these two situations: mobilizing the help of others versus recruiting your own internal resources (in order to implement a desired solution).

When we need external help: using the three sources of energy to implement a decision

There are three sources of energy that, when used correctly, can implement a decision and deliver change. The sources are: authority, power, and influence.

What is authority?

Authority is a person's right to decide on something (accepted by all the relevant people). And by "decide" we mean the **right** to say yes AND no.

If I ask my kids to help me with my diet and not leave junk food all over the place, it may go like this:

"Kids, please, I don't want to see any junk food in the house. Eat it somewhere else."
"But Daddy, the fun is to eat it while we are playing Xbox."
"I said no."
"Why?"
"Because I'm you dad and I said so!"

What is this dad doing? Invoking his authority. This is a right that parents have, at least theoretically, to say "yes" and "no" to their kids.

Below, I have depicted authority as a circle because there is a limit to your right to say "yes" and "no." Inside the circle you have authority. Outside of the circle you do not have authority. If you decide or authorize any change beyond the border of the circle you are abusing your authority.

Maybe invoking your authority will suffice. Maybe that will be enough to make your kids cooperate. But what if your spouse is the cookie culprit? In the case of spouses, neither one has authority over the other unless it is spelled out upfront—like, who decides how to decorate the house, or who decides what time dinner is served—usually the authority is shared.

Authority also has limits. It may not be sufficient to simply invoke it in an attempt to make other people cooperate and help you implement your solution.

If invoking your authority has failed, you may be tempted to look to the second source of energy to get the cooperation you need: power.

What is power?

Power is the **capability**, not the right, to punish and/or reward. If I can give you what you want or cherish (reward you by giving something to you), or hurt you by withholding what you want (punish you), then I have power over you.

To withhold an **<u>expected</u>** reward is a punishment. You expect something. You believe you have earned it. You deserve it. If it is denied to you, you are hurt. You feel you were, by default, punished.

So in trying to implement his solution with his children, the parent in the example above, can threaten:

"You either cooperate, or I'll take the Xbox away and won't let you play."

If they still don't cooperate after he takes the Xbox, the parent can increase the punishments.

"And on top of that, now you'll be grounded for a week."

This is an example of Authorized Power. The parent has the authority to take the Xbox, and also the power to ground the children.

Now assume a different situation: the spouse that plays computer games in bed every night. No more pillow talk. Sex life and intimacy suffer.

Neither party has the authority to decide if a spouse can do this, so to change the situation you must either use power or influence.

You might threaten your spouse with some lack of cooperation on your part unless they cooperate.

However, the use of power is not recommended. Why? Because the problem with power is that the more you use it, the less effective it becomes, and the stronger the measures you need to take to obtain the same results. Along the way you destroy your relationships with the very people you need cooperation from.

And that highlights the need for a third energy component, which is Influence.

What is Influence?

The third source of energy that can be used to get things done is influence. Influence happens when we convince the person we need cooperation from to do something without using either authority or power, and that person agrees to cooperate. How can this happen? He or she becomes convinced. You convince them with arguments that make sense.

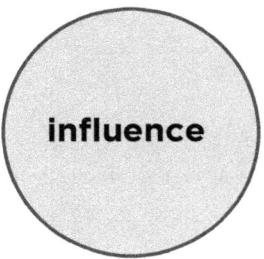

For that, for the influence to be sustainable, you must know the subject on which you are trying to convince someone. Ideally, you will convince the other party that you have common interests in solving the problem, and that the outcome will be good for them too. Also important is that you speak nonjudgmentally, without shaming. And lastly, you must truly give the other person the right to reject your proposal if they so choose. No hard feelings.

How the three circles of energy overlap:

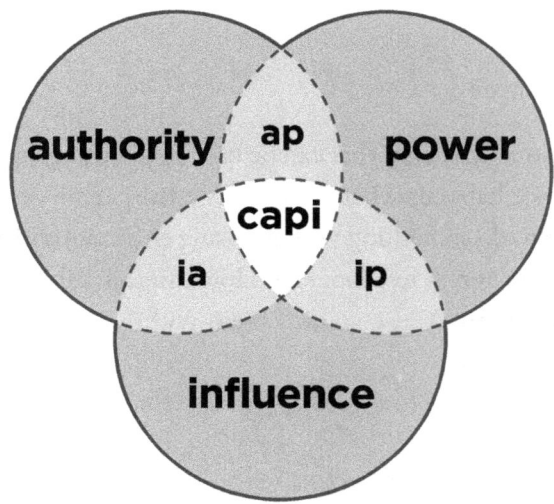

Notice that there are now seven sources of energy:

- Authority
- Authorized Power (ap)
- Power
- Indirect Power (ip)
- Influence
- Accepted Influence (ai)
- CAPI

In addition to Authority, Power, and Influence, the diagram above reveals four additional areas:

- Authorized Power (ap): Authority without power means you have the authority to tell someone what to do, but if they don't do it, you can't really do anything about it. Authorized power, on the other hand, means that if you tell someone what to do and they don't do it, you can punish them (or if they comply, you can reward them).

- Indirect Power (ip): If somebody tries to influence you, and you don't feel you have the freedom to decline their request, that person has indirect power over you. You instinctively read their influence as a threat, as power. To say it another way, when you read between the lines, even if your influencer was nonthreatening, you realize that you had better do what as he or she says. When you think of the request or suggestion the influencer has made, you feel scared. Imagine you have a tough grandfather, the kind that everyone in the family fears. He sees you playing with the grill in the backyard and suggests that you stop. He is not your father or mother, so you don't see him as having direct authority over you, but nonetheless you feel that if you don't do as he says, you may "pay a price."

- Accepted Influence (ai) Here the person with authority has the right to tell you what to do, and can also convince others of the validity of what he or she says. That's when we say, "My father knows what he's talking about. I think he's right and I'm going to do what he says." That's accepted authority.

- CAPI: When authority, power, and influence overlap, you get a new combination. I call this CAPI. The "C" stands for "coalesced." When you have CAPI, you have coalesced authority, power, and influence. You have the authority to tell people what to do. You can also influence them as to the validity of what you want done, and if their actions are delayed or they do not listen well, you have the power to punish or reward them. This assures that they will listen and comply. There is no reason, when you have CAPI, why people would not follow your decisions. You have the authority to make requests or give orders, they know you have the power to punish and reward, and they believe that your wishes are the right ones. You have control.

So if you need cooperation from others, and they know you are in control (i.e., you have the authority to make decisions, and they are convinced of why to follow you but also somewhat concerned about disobeying you), then you have CAPI and you can expect to have their full cooperation. In the Xbox example, it would look something like this: You have the right to tell your kids what to do, and your spouse will not challenge your decision. You have the capability to convince your kids to stop leaving packages of cookies laying around, because if they do not obey, you will punish them by removing their Xbox.

These **seven sources of energy** that cause implementation to happen, I have named **Authorance**.

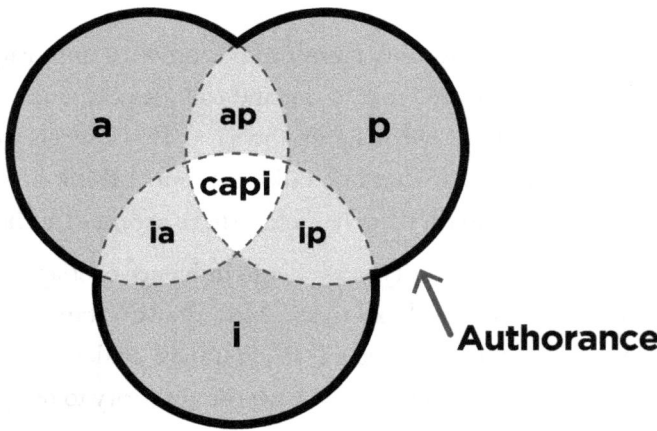

Consider a mother who is trying to persuade her child to eat spinach. She uses different components of *Authorance*. In the beginning she might say "Eat this, it's good for you. Popeye eats spinach, and you can see how strong he is. You will be like Popeye." She is using the influence component of her *authorance*. If the child still refuses to eat, she might allude to the father who will soon be home and will have a present for him but only if he eats.

The use of indirect power may cause the child to eat the spinach. If, however, he still refuses to eat, the mother might get angry and punish him. If according to the value standards of the family, and her spouse does not criticize her for the decision she made, the punishment is acceptable, she is invoking authorized power. If not, she is using power without authority. Perhaps the child still refuses to eat. At this point, the mother might make the classic management mistake: She may resort to pleading. "Why don't you listen to your mother? Why don't you ever do what I tell you to do?" She is using the last resort of her authorance, which is authority. That's tactically wrong. Once she invokes her authority, there is nothing left for an encore. It's fruitless when she says, "Why don't you listen to me? Am I not your mother?" Is it news to the child that she is his mother? How does she think this can be effective? You know you are in trouble if you find yourself offering reminders you shouldn't have to make!

What the mother might use more effectively is *influencing authority*. She, herself, could eat spinach in front of the child, serving as a behavioral model. There is a chance that the child might choose to emulate her.

The mother has CAPI when she suggests "How about eating some spinach?" and the child eats it because he believes it's good for him, he worries about the repercussions of not eating it, and he respects his mother's suggestions.

When we need internal help: Self-CAPI

Interestingly, most problems in implementation are not CAPI over other people, but due to a lack of CAPI over ourselves. "My mind has the right to decide to go on a diet (Authority), but my taste buds will make me miserable if I don't eat that cake (Power). And different parts of my mind are trying to persuade me (Influence): "It will be good for your health not to eat that cake." Internally, I am in conflict.

How do you solve that inner conflict? How do you achieve Self-CAPI, so the decision is implemented in full?

Kahneman and Tversky's research[8] showed that the human mind is actually split in two, and one part (which they called System 2) observes the other (System 1). System 2 also observes our body impulses and our emotions. System 1 (our regular mind) is analogous to Authority, while System 2 (our observing mind, which thinks more slowly and acts as a separate entity beyond the regular mind (System 1), and attempts to persuade both the regular mind and the body) corresponds to Influence. And that's where the true power of free will resides: in our ability to decide with System 2, and do the right thing in spite of being drawn by mind, body, or emotional impulses to do the opposite. Self-restraint is a muscle, and the more we exercise it, the stronger it becomes. The stronger this muscle, the stronger our Self-CAPI will become, and the more it will be available to us to use when we want to implement our decisions.

What, then, is the challenge? Kahneman discovered that System 2 takes effort: influence takes effort. The more you exercise your influence, even on yourself, the more tired you become. This can wear you down throughout the course of a day. If you have a difficult challenge in the morning—something that consumes a significant amount of your energy and free will—it will be more difficult for you to stick to your diet in the evening. This also explains why some parts of you won't "cooperate" in the implementation of your decisions. The non-cooperative parts of you have depleted energy, which in turn reduces your Self-CAPI.

---

8. Kahneman, D. (2011) *Thinking: Fast and Slow*, New York. NY: Farrar, Strauss and Giroux.

Now, who is this wise influential part of you, anyway? Who is influencing you from within your own mind? It's your best self. Remember earlier in the book, when I asked you:

If you had a magic pill that ensured you would act in an integrated fashion, with the four voices in your head in harmony (in other words: if you didn't have any confusion regarding what to do, how to do it, when to do it, with whom to do it, and why you should do it),9 and you were acting from your best self, with total self-trust and self-respect, how many of these PIPs would be solved?

That was a reference to that part of you where hope resides—the part of you that has the potential to be integrated. A person that is "together" has this muscle well developed. We need to nurture that part of ourselves continuously, so it lives in a state of self-trust and self-respect.

If ever you are wondering what to do, the guideline for making a choice is: Will it increase or decrease my self-respect? Will it increase or decrease my trust in myself?

Integration is based on mutual, and in this case, "self," respect and trust. There is no sustainable integration without respect and trust.

A little reminder before Part 4

This concludes Part 3 of the book, which contained the "First, Grow Yourself" self-coaching component of Adizes Coaching. Remember that internal integration always comes first. You'll need to work continuously on your own personal growth, not only for your own well-being, but especially if you want to contribute and help others grow.

---

9. See Part 2, "Foundational Tool #2, How we make decisions: the four voices in our head," for a more in-depth discussion on healthy decision-making and the imperatives required to make a complete decision.

I recommend that you review Part 3 of the book often. As the Adizes Methodology teaches: "Spend twenty-nine days integrating externally, working in the world, and two days fixing the inside." Work on the outside, and self-coach and integrate on the inside. In this way, your self-coaching will function as a monthly tune-up to see what subsystems got misaligned, and you will have the opportunity to get yourself back "together."

Part 4:

How to coach others with Adizes

In Part 3 we learned the Adizes Systemic Coaching Framework for coaching ourselves. But what if you want to coach others and help them develop and grow? In this part of the book, we will introduce you to the best practices for how to use the framework learned in Part 3 when you coach other people.

TRADITIONAL COACHING APPROACHES: THE ONE-SIZE-FITS-ALL TRAP

People are different. You cannot coach them all in the same way. What works with one person may not work with another. If you want to be effective as a coach you need to understand these differences.

As we have made evident throughout this book, the Adizes Methodology (using its PAEI model), helps us understand the differences between people by showing us the four key personality styles and orientations.

The power of PAEI for personal growth lies not only in its ability to identify each of the personality styles (and prescribe the best ways to communicate and establish rapport with each of them), but also in that the PAEI roles are both a personal growth tool and an organizational tool. This personality theory is able to simultaneously describe both the behavioral part (to understand how people behave) and also how behavior driven by needs evolve through a lifecycle. This theory is able to explain what is it that can make both an individual and his or her projects (their company, their job, their family, etc.) healthy. And show you the gaps between who you are and what you are able to perform, and what your life projects really need you to perform in their current stage of evolution. That's because the very same functions that make you healthy as a person can make your projects healthy (i.e., effective and efficient in the short and the long run).

As a person, you can use PAEI to measure how effective and efficient you are, and then determine which particular PAEI roles you need to build up in order to perform dynamically in your current lifecycle stage. The methodology recognizes the fact that our roles and responsibilities in life change as we move along the lifecycle curve. This requires us to grow and develop more PAEI "vitamins," and in some areas (such as parenting), to complement ourselves with others who are strong in the PAEI roles in which we do not excel. In other words, coaching using PAEI is uniquely effective because it matches the person with the "job description."

Most traditional coaching schools miss this point and inadvertently promote a "one-size-fits-all," canned approach. Moreover, people who teach coaching often also fail to identify their own PAEI orientation. For instance, "results-oriented coaching" emphasizes the (P) role over anything else, and they hand out their productivity/speed/execution approach to everyone, without taking into account that this could be too aggressive and ineffective with some coachees (particularly an (I) or (A) person). These types of coaching methods go too fast, too quickly—full speed ahead—trying to "ignite" the coachee, only to find themselves facing great resistance. The reverse is also true: (I)-oriented coaches try to go by the dictum of "first build the relationship." Try this with a (P) coachee and you will lose them in the first session.

So in order to be able to coach and help your coachees break through, you need precise guidelines that take into account these personality differences. You need to know how to communicate with each personality style throughout your coaching conversations. And this is what the following chapters are about.

BEFORE YOU COACH OTHERS, YOU MUST DISCOVER YOUR OWN COACHING PERSONALITY.

As we learned in Part 3, self-awareness is one of the main keys to personal development, not only in terms of self-growth, but also when using your abilities to help others.

Your own personality style may prove to be a great asset when coaching others. If you are a (P) coach you can help a coachee take prompt action and implement a decision.

But this same asset may also become a liability: as a (P) coach, you may become impatient with slower-paced coachees.

That's why it's so important to understand your personality style before you go on to coach others, so you are aware of your strengths as well as your blind spots.

The power of Adizes Coaching lies in this dual-listening strategy: On one hand, you are listening to your coachee. On the other, you are also listening to yourself. This allows you to monitor what's going on in your own mind when you are coaching other people, to adapt your responses according to the coachee's style, and to prevent your own dominant style from taking over. The latter can be detrimental to your coaching: (P) coaches will tend to have a bias toward action—even when that's not the appropriate energy for the coachee in the moment. Likewise, (A) coaches will tend to have a bias toward structure and order, (E)s will emphasize options and possibility, and (I)s will gravitate toward the intra and interpersonal dynamics.

The secret to great coaching is that you yourself can manage your coaching practice according to PAEI principles. So when you coach others, all four PAEI roles are present, assuring the effectiveness and efficiency of the coaching process—whether for short-term, first-order-change coaching or longer-term, second-order change processes.

BENEFITS VS. BLIND SPOTS OF EACH STYLE IN COACHING

The (P) Coach

Strengths:

- Outcome oriented.
- Energetic, works best when coachees are "stuck in their heads" and action is needed.
- Knows how to translate options and ideas into practical solutions.
- Ideal when time is of the essence and there is a need for "quick and dirty" solutions.
- Encourages the coachee to not give up, to keep trying until results are obtained.

Blind Spots:

- May be pushy with clients
- Gives answers (whether in diagnosis or coaching) instead of asking empowering questions to lead to coachees discover solutions by themselves.
- Can become impatient with both coachees and process
- Don't allow experience to develop and become frustrated with the ups and downs of the process
- Can be too directive, may try to impose formulas and shortcuts for rapid success
- Style fits mainly first-order change; may have difficulty working on long-term, second-order change, and with emotionally intense coachees.
- Always getting "right down to business" may alienate sensitive, more interpersonal coachees.

The (A) Coach

Strengths:

- Ethical about coaching standards and values
- Formal, agreement-based style; conducts the coaching process in an orderly way
- Strong analytical and diagnostic skills
- Encourages coachee to be responsible and commit to the process
- Works well with frameworks and coaching protocols
- Good when a coachee needs structure and routine building in their life
- Helps coachee prioritize and organize their life
- Helps coachee with time management and other (A)dministrative skills

Blind Spots:

- May adopt a rigid approach
- May be too slow
- Too much time diagnosing and collecting information on the coachee
- May inhibit the coachee's spontaneity
- Low creativity; won't encourage adventurous dreaming and brainstorming

The (E) Coach

Strengths:

- Best for helping coachee optimistically and creatively brainstorm possibilities and options.
- Models for the coachee how to find new ways to look at things.
- Not accepting of limiting beliefs; chutzpah for challenging the coachee.
- Exciting energy.
- Uses humor.
- Helps coachee to be proactive.
- Helps coachee to reframe negative experiences and turn things around.

Blind Spots:

- Uneasy when a coachee displays pain.
- May unconsciously impose their own agenda.
- Can become impatient with a person who is too negative.

- May become bored with a coachee who gets stuck and doesn't progress.
- Impatient with chronic conditions or temporarily uncoachable people.

The (I) Coach

Strengths:

- Very accepting, inclusive, and validating
- Master of engaged listening.
- Shows belief in the coachee's potential.
- Creates a safe and supportive environment for coachees to open themselves up
- Able to quickly generate trust.
- Helps coachee identify their emotions and feelings and develop emotional intelligence.
- Has empathy and compassion for the coachee's difficulties.
- Can suspend own needs and focus undividedly on the coachee.

Blind Spots:

- May get stuck in the coachee's emotional pain and forget to move on.
- Unable to "keep the eye on the ball" and stay solution focused
- Reads too much into situations.
- May have difficulty setting good boundaries.

AND ONE MORE THING BEFORE YOU GO AND COACH: REMEMBER TO SWITCH TO LISTENING MODE.

A basic coaching tenet is that coachees already have inside of them the resources to solve their problems. Coaches who listen deeply, and ask open-ended questions, show that they trust their coachee and believe they will find the answers to their challenges.

Before you begin any coaching session, I recommend that you put a piece of paper in front of you with a big question mark on it. It will remind you to ask questions instead of giving advice or solutions. The ideal ratio is 80/20: The coachee talks 80% of the time, and you talk 20% of the time. The paper will remind you that you are in coaching mode, and that you are not a consultant who gives out advice. This is a great way to ensure that your coachees will arrive at their own conclusions.

If your coachee suggests a solution to a problem that you think is not a good one, do not jump to tell them why it's bad or what they might do differently. Ask them what will happen if they implement their decision. Steer them to look at the potential downsides of their solution—so that they, themselves, arrive at the conclusion that their solution may not be the best one. One way to do that is to ask them : What will happen if you implement your decision? What will happen and let them realize the potential drawbacks. The collateral damage the solution might cause.

What if they get stuck on a question, and cannot answer it? If they say, "I don't know." The next step is to brainstorm the options together. Classical coaching questions such as, "What would you do if you did know?" or "What would a person you admire do in this situation?" or "How would your ideal self act in a situation like this?" can help the coachee get unstuck.

Good coaches also make deliberate use of silence. If the subject gets "heavy," you may stay silent and allow the coachee to process the information. Always let them speak first. Inexperienced coaches get performance anxiety and try to fill the air because they feel very uncomfortable with silence. Get comfortable with silence, so that your coachee's can use it to arrive at their solutions.

Your one-on-one coaching sessions should always be conducted in a relaxed setting, at a quiet place, with no interruptions. No time pressure whatsoever. This is conducive to creating an environment of listening, trust, and respect.

Begin your sessions in a casual way, asking the coachee how they are doing and what they want to work on in the session.[1] Trigger those questions and become silent, allowing them to speak freely. The less you talk, the better.

Some coachees may use the initial exchange at the beginning of the session as an opportunity to unload strong emotions. Sometimes these can be family-related or deal with issues within their relationships. Remember that coaches are not consultants and that they don't give advice. While it's okay to listen and show sympathy,[2] you should refrain from giving family advice.[3]

---

1. With (P) coachees, as will be shown in the upcoming section, the initial warm-up and exchange should be kept to a minimum, and you should move quickly to the practical coaching portion of the session.
2. Not empathy, though. In empathy you identify with their pain and start sharing your own pain to show them they are not alone. The more you start identifying yourself with their pain, the more you lose your role as the coach, and cannot coach. You cannot see the picture when you are in it.
3. If you choose to refer your coachee to a family therapist, only do so if the therapist is certified in Adizes, in the theory at a minimum. Otherwise their methodology might be incompatible with the Adizes methodology and it will only confuse the coachee.

HOW TO COACH THE DIFFERENT PAEI STYLES[4]

Ask coaching questions that encourage learning

Coaching has its roots in socratic dialogue, and so your goal as a coach is to help coachees discover their own solutions. This is especially important when you seem to discover a "clear solution" to the coachee's problem due to his or her particular PAEI personality style.

For example, when dealing with a (P) style, imagine the coachee is telling you about a problem she had with her spouse, when she got very impatient and irritated due to his slower pace of doing things. Instead of asking "what are you missing as you rush through the days/weeks of your life?", which refers directly to her personality style in a negative way, you could ask: "what could have been done differently?". The latter question invites possibility and encourages the coachee to explore options. It implies that perhaps, the (P) way may be appropriate sometimes, and at other times a different strategy may be more adequate.

Other questions that are generic -you don't address the coachee's personality style directly- are:

- In what ways you approached tasks/people this week?[5]
- What were the benefits and the cons of your approach?
- If you were acting from your best-self, how could you have approached this situation differently? (here in the example above, the coachee could reply: "I could have been more PI,

---

[4]. For an in-depth treatment see also Adizes, I. *Leading the Leaders: How to Enrich Your Style of Management and Handle People Whose Style Is Different from Yours*. Santa Barbara, CA: Adizes Institute Publications, 2004.

[5]. Coach should have gone through a proper brief introduction of basic Adizes terms so the coachee becomes familiar with them, and can identify the different PAEI approaches to task and people.

and gently communicate I was in a hurry, instead of my pure (P) approach of becoming dismissive and impatient.

By now you know your own coaching style, how it will relate to your coachees, and what is the right disposition and mindset for beginning the coaching session . Next, we will look at how to adapt your coaching to different styles of people.

HOW TO COACH THE (P) STYLE

First, create rapport: match the (P)'s personality frequency

In order to create rapport with a (P)-style coachee, you need to take into account their fast-paced, impatient, and hurried manner. To relate best to this style, follow these guidelines:

- Be straightforward, don't beat around the bush.
- No warmups. Many coaches believe that before you start any coaching work you need to first "create the relationship." That's not necessary with the (P) style. This may sound counterintuitive to some coaches, especially the (I)s among them, but if there is a surefire way to lose a (P) coachee, it is by not getting right to the point. They will get annoyed and lose interest.
- Always stay practical. Don't be theoretical. Show the pragmatic application of everything you say.
- Provide "deliverables" at regular intervals (every fifteen minutes or so), so they feel the "take home value" of the coaching.

The diagnosis stage with a (P) style

(P)s typically have very little patience for doing coaching work. Moreover, there may not even be a perception of the need for coaching.

Why? Because (P)s don't understand the language of prevention and development. The only way they may begin to understand the need for coaching is if there is already a crisis.

What this means is that there will likely be a notable resistance to the process, right from the beginning. You may not even be able to start the process unless you can get the (P) to set aside any distractions and try to focus on the coaching work.

If, whether motivated by a crisis[6] or not, the (P) finally agrees to accept coaching, it's important that you are aware of a couple of misconceptions that Ps often have, which will need to be addressed.

- Misconception #1: "But there is no time to be coached!"
- Misconception #2: "There must be a faster solution"

Let's address these misconceptions.

"But there is no time to be coached!" (P)s live with the sense that they can't stop to think. It's as if the only thing they value is doing. Thinking is a waste of time, time that could be put into doing. If a person's health is at risk, or they have very bad personal habits that are impacting their quality of life (and/or the lives of the people who live with them), it would be wise to stop and revisit their life strategies. But … (P)s prefer to improvise: "If it works, fine! That's it! Boom! Let's go!"

> *"One of my weaknesses is impatience. I just have this aching need to get great things done. Can't stand slow change."* —Robin Sharma

---

6. If the case is that they didn't "feel" there was a crisis, then they were probably sent to you by a spouse or parent. You need to make them take ownership of the problem. Try to leverage them by asking, "If you do nothing, what do you think will happen with your problem?" If the answer is "nothing," then they don't see the need to change, and the sessions will be a waste of time. Ask them to come back when they feel the need to change.

The word "strategize" may cause an allergic reaction in these coachees. They may come to you and say, "OK, what is the solutioin? What do I need to do? Just tell me what needs to be done so we can finish up here." Which brings us to the second misconception.

"There must be a faster solution." Because of their impatience, perhaps the most difficult thing to convey to a (P) type is that coaching is a process, not an event. Moreover, a (P) focuses only on the end result. Did we win or did we lose? If we won then we celebrate, and if we lost then we hide our faces. I saw this very clearly when I consulted with sports teams. For a typical (P), the only thing that counts is winning. Vince Lombardi used to say "Winning isn't everything. It's the only thing." That's the (P) mentality. But in personal growth, this is a very limiting assumption.

> *"Keep going and don't give up when you don't see progress. If you are on a diet, your data may not yet show progress (no change in pants size), but it's proving process (you keep conditioning yourself into a healthier lifestyle, going every day to the gym, and you keep eating healthy)."* —Jon Acuff

When people try to stick to a coaching plan and try to improve themselves, sometimes it can get very tough. But failure is a tremendous opportunity to learn, and to become better. And eventually people with this attitude will win.

If a person looks only at results, they are like a child with a new musical instrument. The child might insist on playing fast, even though playing too fast before mastering the form—the notes, the fingering, the chords—means they will make a lot of mistakes.

To help a (P) grow, we encourage them to slow down and learn to play the instrument correctly from the start—to learn proper form and technique. The function of playing at the appropriate speed will inevitably follow. For a (P), function is all-important. "Let's play," they insist, even before they've learned the basic form.

In other words, it's key that they don't focus exclusively on the solution, but also on the process for arriving at that solution. Arriving at the right solution via the wrong process, in the long run, is worse than arriving at the wrong solution via the right process. The wrong process will only lead to the right solution by sheer luck—and therefore will not be repeatable in the coachee's life—whereas the right process will eventually bring the right result and have lasting impact in the long run.

Setting coaching goals with the (P) style

Coaching can really help the (P) type expand their horizons. When setting coaching goals with a (P) person, their focus will typically be on the short term. That's where they excel. It's as if they shout at life: "Just give me a task to do now!" But what about the long run? They may be tempted to proudly paraphrase John Maynard Keynes when he was asked that same question and replied: "In the long run we are all dead." Such is their rejection of anything beyond the immediate.

The values of (P) people: what's important to the (P) coachee

When coaching a (P) person it's important to always remember their values—the issues and principles that are important to them, that are central in their life.

Here is a list of their *toward* values (the things they most seek to achieve):

results, practicality, speed, achievement, completion, getting things done, clarity in communication

Here is a list of the things they try to *avoid*:

slowness, idleness, open loops, theories, big ideas, talking instead of doing, the human aspects that interfere with getting things done, the need to stop for anything that is not (P) (that is, dedicating time to (A), (E), or (I); vague/indirect communication).

The Limiting Beliefs of the (P) coachee: and the lenses through which they see the world

The (P) mindset is sustained by a series of limiting beliefs. In coaching we bring awareness to these beliefs, so the (P) individual can become conscious of them. Remember that self-observation is the foundation for self-adjustment. As the quote I included in Part 1 of this book, by R.D. Laing, says: *"The range of what we think and do is limited by what we fail to notice. And because we fail to notice that we fail to notice, there is little we can do to change; until we notice how failing to notice shapes our thoughts and deeds."*

"We repeat what we don't repair." —Christine Langley

Let's take a look at some of the most stifling beliefs that the (P) style holds:

"Let's find a quick solution!"

(P)s want to solve everything right now, today! They see a problem, and they want to fix it. They can't bear to leave a problem unattended.

But sometimes it may simply be too early to deal with a problem, and the most immediate solution may only seem to be to try to solve it. In fact, a quickie solution may only disguise the problem, and eventually just exacerbate it.

As we have stated repeatedly, (P)s just want a simple solution. Simple. Quick. Done. But life is far from simple. It's not always best to hurry and fix something hastily. We must take the time to correctly assess what the problem is, then distinguish between solving, relieving, or arresting it.

"People won't move unless they are shoved."

If (P)s want to make something happen, they don't apply gentle pressure, they shove. Why? Because (P)s are always dealing with some kind of crisis. It is as if they enjoy the adrenaline rush, so they create time pressures and crises to get that adrenaline going. This is because they often confuse quantity with quality. As if more is better.

But there are consequences to this way of thinking and living. When there is time pressure, there is a perceived need to act quickly.

The coach's role is to help the (P) become aware that not everything is a crisis … and not everything needs to be a crisis. Is the situation really a crisis, or do they just want to get it over with as soon as possible? In other words, did their behavior make it a crisis?

Easy does it. The purpose of the coaching in this regard is to help the coachee see that there is no need to push everything along, every time. There is no need to be overbearing. When they are creating crises, the amount of energy they are expending to get people to act is way out of proportion to what is necessary or appropriate.

"We need to try harder!"

When things don't work, (P)s believe the solution is to double the efforts—put on the blinders and push full speed ahead. But what if the direction they are taking is the wrong one to begin with?

> *"All movement is not forward."* —Ellen Glasgow

Imagine a (P) is trying to change the ink in the printer. They may open the lid and push on the old cartridge, only to find that it won't come out. In the same situation, an (A) may look in the printer's manual to find the correct procedure for removing the cartridge, but the (P) may just push harder (to try to get that darn cartridge out). Notice how there is no change in strategy on the (P)'s part, no trying of a different solution. They need to learn that if what they are doing is not working, then they need to STOP and ask themselves whether or not they are doing the right thing.

> *"Things alter for the worse spontaneously, if they be not altered for the better designedly."* —Francis Bacon

"Let's fix this right now!"

A (P) person is crisis-oriented, meaning that what gets a (P)'s attention is the squeaking wheel. (P)s can get overly involved in small things, losing track of the big picture. Whether in their personal or professional lives, they can get caught up in the tactical decisions, which causes them to miss the strategic decisions.

But not every squeaking wheel has to be addressed right here and now. Sometimes waiting can be the right thing to do. Why? Because there are bigger fish to fry.

Michael asked his friend Mary to help him with his home-internet connection. He'd been getting brief interruptions in his Wi-Fi which was making him very nervous. Mary couldn't find a solution and so Michael got very frustrated and tried to fix the problem himself—trying again and again to fix it with no success—working incessantly on his internet connection and forgetting his other priorities and obligations along the way.

Now, how do (P)s abuse time? They want to do everything right now. Their view of time is that it should be used to solve immediate problems. As a result, they do not set priorities, and they avoid long-range planning. They have no concern for problems that are "five years down the pike."

But the truth is that not everything is a crisis, and not everything has to be done immediately. Sometimes priorities need to be set before action is taken.

"Let's find a shortcut!"

A (P) is always looking for the simplest solution or shortcut. Because of this tendency, they can inadvertently make a situation more complicated, because the remedy they come up with may be so flawed that it's worse than the disease they are trying to cure.

Complex problems are like a tangled ball of string. How do we unravel it? Carefully. Slowly. We have to think about interdependencies and boundaries. We pull gently on one string until there is resistance. Then we loosen the string that is obstructing the first one. Then we return to the first string and continue loosening it, etc.

(P)s find such methodical slowness disturbing. They are impatient. When they encounter resistance, they simply pull harder. And what happens? Pulling on the strings only twists them together more tightly. Sometimes they give up and cut the string apart with a knife; they just whack at it—finished!

In coaching there is a **short/long way,** and a **long/short way.** For example, if I am in unknown territory, and there is a normal route to lead me out—but it is long—taking the long route can prove to be "shorter" than trying to find a shortcut and getting lost.

In the same way, what may appear to be a long coaching process is actually going to produce a decision in the end that can be easily and quickly implemented. A slow process may result in a good decision and fast implementation, while a quick decision (made without sufficient attention to detail), may produce a long and arduous implementation.

"There is no time to brainstorm and evaluate different alternatives. Let's not make this complicated!"

Problem-solving in coaching is like stepping into a maze. We must think before we take each step, and sometimes we have to go back and refind our way.

It's OK that we don't know everything up front. It's also OK that the process of exploring is not very effective or efficient in the short run. We make many false starts. We spend some time eliminating alternatives. But this isn't time wasted. We actually learn something during this process. We learn what is not applicable or appropriate.

Our goal is to encourage the (P) to explore. To learn. To find out what they do not know. Then, at least, they'll know that they don't know. That would be a very important discovery for them. The next most important discovery would be to cool it and learn to stay calm in the face of uncertainty. We've found out that we don't know something; now let's find out what we need to know in order to achieve our goal.

HOW TO COACH THE (A) STYLE

First, create rapport: match the (A)'s personality frequency

In order to create rapport with an (A)-style coachee, you need to take into account their structured manner. To relate best to this style, follow these guidelines:

- Organize your session well. From the beginning, come from a place of structure, developing the conversation, and plan a succinct closure for the end of the session.
- Be systematic.
- Adopt a step-by-step approach.

- Establish clear rules for the coaching process. Sign a proper coaching agreement.
- Set clear expectations.
- Clarify commitments and obligations for both the coach and the coachee.
- Keep your promises.
- Last but not least, always be on time!

The diagnosis stage with an (A) style

"Productivity is never an accident. It is always the result of a commitment to excellence, intelligent planning, and focused effort." —Paul Meyer

If with the (P) style we found a general impatience and a desire to rush things, with the (A) style we find quite the opposite tendency: a will to think things through thoroughly and meticulously. A thorough diagnosis of the problem will be very appreciated by the (A) style coachee. So take your time. Don't hurry.

When you ask an (A), "What is the problem?" they will usually start back with Adam and Eve, "In the beginning …"—and give you the whole history of the problem.

Having this 2000+ years perspective of the problem, how long do they think it will take to solve it? Another few thousand years, of course.

An (A) perceives every problem as very complicated, very big, and very overwhelming; they see the problem in the past and the solution somewhere vaguely in the future. With such time span it will take forever to make anything happen. I call this "paralysis from over analysis."

What actually needs to happen is to dedicate appropriate time to do the diagnosis, and then move on. I emphasize the word 'appropriate' because (A) types are tempted to dedicate too much time to thinking about and understanding root causes. They may get caught up in too many details, and overemphasize process, often at the expense of doing and getting results.

In other words, the idea is not to focus only on the process. Encourage them to focus on the right process for arriving at a solution but then shift to execution. Even a longtime problem with deep roots may not need a big, complicated solution. In fact, sometimes, to gain time, it makes sense to alleviate some of the symptoms quickly, and deal with the longer-term issues later on.

Setting coaching goals with the (A) style

Because they are detail-oriented people, coaching can help the (A) style think outside of their own box. Their preoccupation with details sometimes causes them to lose sight of the big picture. They lack vision. Coaching can help them clarify a greater vision for their personal and professional lives.

The values of (A) people: what's important to the (A) coachee

In a coaching process with an (A) coachee it's important to always remember their values: the issues and principles that are important to them, that are central in their life.

Here is a list of their toward values (the things they most seek to achieve):

efficiency, order, structure, doing things right, rules, enforcement, responsibility, organization, neatness, cleanliness, good manners, predictability

Here is a list of the things they try to avoid:

disorganization, lack of precision, sloppiness, carelessness, impoliteness, impropriety, transgression, risk

The Limiting Beliefs of the (A) coachee: and the lenses through which they see the world

The (A) mindset is sustained by a series of limiting beliefs. In coaching we bring awareness to these beliefs, in order to help the (A)-oriented person can become conscious of them. So here are some of the most crippling beliefs that the (A) style holds:

"The form will produce the function."

How can we tell when form is dysfunctional and when it isn't? When we follow the form, and it doesn't produce the results we anticipated, we need to check the how part of the process. Maybe what we are doing and why we are doing it are fine, but the how is undermining our results.

We may be tempted to believe, for example, that an orderly apartment produces a healthier person—and therefore feel the need to overemphasize the importance of cleaning. There is some truth to this statement, but is it always the case? Or is it necessarily the case? Isn't it true that it's absolutely possible to actually become unhealthy by obsessing about order and cleanliness? Well, this is often the case for many (A) people, losing sight of what is important in life due to going overboard with rules and order.

So, a simple solution may seem to be just to pull the cleaning (or the rituals of cleaning) back to a reasonable amount, and yet this simple-sounding solution often proves to be anything but simple. It's precisely our long-established habits—our "hows"—that are the most difficult to change. The "how" also depends on one's personal style, which is almost impossible to change, especially when one is under stress.

We help the (A) coachee remember that form does not necessarily produce the desired results. And we encourage them to check and validate whether the form they have chosen is actually working. If it is not, then they may want to change it.

"It is possible to obtain 100% control over something."

An (A) wants complete control and will spend an enormous amount of time and energy trying to attain it.

For example, an (A) may obsess about health. And they may go to every extreme in their diet, subjecting everybody around them to every detail. "Hold it! What dressing did you use on that salad? Oh, no! That will give me twenty extra calories today! I told you a thousand times to be more careful!" What the (A) is missing by being obsessive and argumentative, is that emotional tension and fights are not good for weight loss either. When we release cortisol (which happens when we are under stress), we produce fat and gain weight. So, biologically speaking, the cost of fighting over the dressing on the salad (and in typical (A) fashion, a feeling of resentment that may linger for a few hours or days) does more damage than the twenty calories would have given the (A) anyway. In their search for perfection, the (A) often tries to control every single detail and the cost of establishing such controls may sometimes exceed the value they thought they were seeking.

"In the face of uncertainty, it's always best to wait , not act prematurelly."

An (A), like a (P), abhors ambiguity. But while a (P) will do anything, even the wrong thing, rather than wait for clarity, an (A) will wait forever, not comprehending that inaction in times of change can be worse than ambiguity. Unlike an (E), an (A) cannot interpret clues in the fog. He will always prefer to hold out for certainty. The danger, of course, is that by the time a trend becomes certain, the opportunity may have been lost.

> *"I was deeply in love with her. But I never told her. I was not sure what her reaction would be. Would she say yes? No? And then she got married to someone else. One day, after 25 years, she told me that back then she was in love with me too, but because I never proposed, she ended up marrying someone else."* —Ricardo Darin, "The Secret in Their Eyes"

We help the (A) coachee understand that computing risk does not mean rejecting it altogether. Uncertainty is part of the process; they have to learn to live with it and even to welcome it. Without risk, there is no opportunity. Without opportunity, there is no chance of success.

If ambiguity is not the worst evil, then what is? Without a doubt, for an (A) it is inaction in times of change.

> *"There are risks and costs to a program of action. But they are far less than the long-range risks and costs of comfortable inaction."* —John F. Kennedy

"There are rules for making progress in life."

(A)s have a disease called "manualitis": They live their lives according to manuals, precedents, and rules. Whether these are manuals created by them or by other people and then followed by the (A), it's very difficult for the (A) to not stick to the set of rules they have chosen.

At the onset of the COVID-19 pandemic, (A)s everywhere were heard saying, "We can't possibly just switch to online learning. Nothing can replace traditional in-person classes. What? Start tomorrow? Impossible! We won't be able to learn. How long will this last? How can classes be converted that fast? We've never tried this before! This format can't possibly work. We haven't studied it. We need time to create a format!" The sudden and urgent shift to online learning, worldwide, in early 2020 was unprecedented, and therefore unpracticed and unstudied. A perfect storm for an (A) type—whether teacher or parent or student—to be completely panicked and stressed, pointing out the flaws and getting lost in their fears, rather than looking for the opportunities. Why? Because "it has not been proven yet that it works."

What the (A) has so much trouble seeing is that sometimes in real life, we may have to violate some of our efficiency rules when we need to respond quickly and be effective in unusual situations. We must be willing to be flexible, to allow for deviations from the norm, to take some shortcuts.

"To make progress, the key is to go slow."

An (A) interprets speed with a lack of quality. They move slowly, ponderously. If the coach gives them an assignment that is challenging in that it needs to be done quickly, they may become resistant. They want to go slow. They punctuate everything they say …and take their time. They think about each detail; then they think again.

When (A) types sense confusion, they slow down their speech. Why? They believe if they go slower, what they say will become clearer. But slower doesn't necessarily mean clearer.

> *"There is a slowness in affairs which ripens them, and a slowness which rots them."* —Joseph Roux

"It's a must to be precise."

For an (A), $999,999.50 is not a million; 8:31 is not 8:30. They're very precise, very literal.

Their life may be going in the wrong direction, but any calculation is computed to the third decimal.

Why are they so detail oriented? Because they prefer not to take risks. They want everything to be safe and precise. But their obsession with being precise can cause them ultimately to fail, big-time.

An **(A)** spends an excessive amount of time worrying about details. They prefer to do things right rather than do the right thing. In other words, they would rather be precisely wrong than approximately right. To use a tennis analogy: **(A)s** would probably prefer to wait until they know exactly where the ball is going to land before they are willing to hit it. But by that time, of course, it's too late.

"It's important to be cost-aware."

This is the curse of an (A). They usually don't pay attention to the value of a thing, for the following reason: cost is certain, value is maybe.

For example: Let's say that their profession may be in decline, and someone suggests to the (A) that they update their knowledge with some professional trainings. The first thing the (A) will look at is the cost. "Can I afford this?" An (A) will ask this question before even considering any potential return that the trainings might yield.

It's true that value is less certain than cost. But that doesn't necessarily make value less important. Unless we invest, we cannot obtain a return. Unless we pay attention to value, we risk allowing little if anything to happen around us. In the example above, perhaps this is even the root cause of the problem: the professional decline may have come to the (A) due to a resistance to invest in their own career, because of the costs involved.

We encourage the (A) to evaluate the costs, certainly, but also the probability of success, and to compare the two. We do this to help them learn to give weight to value.

"For a good solution it must have been tested before."

An (A), when presented with a solution in a coaching session, will usually want to know: "Who else has done it this way?" "Where else has this been successful?"

They may also ask their coach about previous coachee successes and requests references.

Of course, if there really is some precedent, if there is some proof that the proposed solution has already worked elsewhere, then it's always nice to learn from another's experience.

But if not, why shouldn't they be the first person to try it?

"Once a decision and a course of action is taken, should not change."

(A)s hate change. They are the opposite of (E)s, who live to make changes. A typical **(A)** will say, "I did a few coaching sessions, I spent the money, I analyzed, and my coach and I decided what to do. So we are not going to revisit this decision anymore."

But why not? Coaching is a dynamic process. New options may appear. We may do trial and error. Everything is a study in progress. Environments change, and thus whatever we decided might have to change down the road. In fact, it is the process of implementation that often causes the change—because as we're implementing, we might discover that some of our decisions were impractical for reasons that couldn't have been foreseen.

We encourage the (A) to watch closely as they implement a decision; to keep their eyes open because they never know for sure what the future will bring.

It's like watching toddlers grow. We can't let them move around without supervision, because we don't know what they will do next. We have to constantly watch. In the same way, decisions may need to change as implementation occurs—not always, but with a high rate of change this is a real probability.

Of course, we also have to make prudent decisions, looking at the cost of change versus the value of change. Either way can be very expensive: too much flexibility versus not enough. The real answer can often be found somewhere in between.

HOW TO COACH THE (E) STYLE

First, create rapport: match the (E)'s personality frequency

In order to create rapport with an (E)-style coachee, you need to take into account their creative, and often disruptive, manner. To relate best to this style, follow these guidelines:

- Stay open to their ideas. Get truly interested in them. Allow them to share. Be patient and provide the listening space.

- Very important consideration: They may go fast. Especially if, in addition to (E), they have a strong (P). They may jump from one subject to the next. It can be a challenge for some (E) type coaches to keep track of what they say.

- Learn how to be patient with their speed. They process things very fast. You will work with them on slowing their pace, but to create rapport, you first need to adjust your own speed to match theirs. This will make it safe for them to express themselves. Without this, you'll break rapport with them.

- Although in general we can say you need to be in charge of the coaching session and give it proper structure, with the (E) don't be too rigid; don't get locked in a predefined plan for the session. Allow them some latitude (of course, with limits) to improvise a bit and follow the path of their quick, creative minds.

- No one should attend the coaching session but the (E) coachee and yourself. (E)s behave very differently when they are in a one-on-one setting versus when there is even one additional person. When the latter happens, their desire for dominance

may be triggered and their resistance to the issues at hand will be highly increased.
- Notice if their eyes go upward as if looking for inspiration, or if they shut them. This signals that they are processing and thinking. Remain quiet and wait for them to come back from wherever their mind has drifted to.

The diagnosis stage with an (E) style

Because of their creative analytical ability, (E)s can spend an inordinate amount of time diagnosing the why and who of a problem, instead of trying to solve it by focusing on the what and how to do. Actual problem-solving would mean leaving behind the intellectual excitement of analysis (on which they thrive), and focusing on the what and the how, which they find boring. Solving a problem also leads to an end, which (E)s perceive as a kind of death.

But diagnosing, discussing, and analyzing problems without focusing on potential solutions is like repeatedly scratching at a small scab: The mild pain gives some pleasure, but eventually the scab bleeds and what was a small cut can become a large wound.

> "For good ideas and true innovation, you need human interaction, conflict, argument, debate."   —Margaret Heffernan

In Israel, a very (E)-style culture, people will often debate a problem until you wonder whether they really want to solve it or if they just enjoy debating it. It's called Talmudism: They start with a small problem, and by the time they finish discussing it a bigger, deeper problem has grown out of the discussion, but often without a finalized solution.

Setting coaching goals with the (E) style

In coaching, when the time comes for setting goals, we need to remember that (E)s are impatient. Their vision and goals are what drives them; once they see the vision, they dismiss the implementation process as just a matter of details. In fact, once they envision an action, for them it's already a done deal, already a reality. (E)s are convinced that if everyone was committed to their vision, we would all move faster.

Thus, they have a problem with timelines. They become unusually optimistic, as they consistently underestimate how long it will take to complete any given task.

Let's say they plan to meet with someone for half an hour to discuss a problem. The length of time that it actually takes is a measure of the magnitude of an (E)'s poor time-measuring skills. I call it their "time bias multiple."

If a goal is to lose ten pounds, and they believe they can do it in one month, but in reality it will take three months, then their bias multiple is three.

Be aware of this disparity between what they expect and what reality might require. Whatever is the plan, it is sure to take longer than they believe it should. In fact, the bigger their (E), the higher off the ground they are (and the wilder their dreams and the stronger their resolve), and it is all the more likely that their bias multiple will be very high.

To get the best sense of their own bias multiple, ask the coachee to talk to their friends, the people they live with, and the people they work with.

The tendency to expect something just because they want it, and the fear that nothing will happen unless they apply pressure and threaten, negatively impacts the (E)'s ability to communicate with others. For this reason, it is crucial to figure out their time bias multiple. Then, once they know by how much they are likely to underestimate, they can correct their expectations upfront.

The values of (E) people: what's important to the (E) coachee

In a coaching process with an (E) coachee it's important to always remember their values—the issues and principles that are important to them, that are central in their lives.

Here is a list of their toward values (the things they most seek to achieve):

impact in the world, immortality, legacy, power, creativity, ideas

Here is a list of the things they try to avoid:

boredom, being irrelevant, not heard, too much detail, criticism of their ideas

The Limiting Beliefs of the (E) coachee: and the lenses through which they see the world

The (E) mindset is sustained by a series of limiting beliefs. In coaching we bring awareness to these beliefs.

Here are some of the most crippling beliefs of the (E) personality:

"Let's keep the excitement going!"

There is an Israeli expression that says, "Speak slowly, for me to understand you fast." Meaning, "It's better to feed people with a teaspoon than with a fire hose."

Because (E)s try to fill their day with a week's worth of work, their minds work faster than their lips can move. They are constantly jumping from one subject to the next, which reminds them of a third. It's not so much the speed of their speech, but their stream-of-consciousness style of speaking that causes (E)s to interrupt their own sentences or forget to complete their thoughts.

This bewilders their listeners. "What the heck is this person trying to get at?" they wonder. "What does he want from me?"

An (E)'s excitement often stimulates other people's thinking, which is a good thing, except that the overstimulated (E) cannot take in what you are trying to add to the conversation. They are too busy processing old inputs (their own thoughts, which they are racing to put into words) to listen to new inputs (anything you are trying to say).

We encourage the (E) to watch carefully when they are in a conversation, to confirm that the person they are speaking to has understood what they are saying, before continuing to speak. If their interlocutor's eyes "go out to lunch," we ask the (E) coachee to stop talking and wait for the person's attention to return. It does no good to talk if no one is listening.

Moreover, if the (E) senses that their interlocutor can't follow their train of thought, we ask the (E) to STOP. Confusion should be taken as a red flag, a warning that the other person doesn't quite understand what the (E) is saying.

"I like to be spontaneous and share ideas as they arise."

(E)s can have ten ideas a minute. And they get excited by their own ideas. Naturally they want to share their enthusiasm and convince others. But because they are so expressive—and in their excitement they tend to speak in an intense and exaggerated style—they can overwhelm not only their coach but their friends, family, and the people they work with. This can cause the coaching process to derail, because as they are very creative they jump form one subject to another and instead of making progress you end up running in circles.

They may share, with great excitement, "I know what I'll do! I'll take that Yoga class! It will be amazing for my concentration and health! I already booked three classes for next week! …" But their friends know that while the (E) may be overly enthusiastic now, by next week they may completely change their mind. Typical expression one can hear an (E) say: "It is too late for you to disagree with me. I already changed my mind."

Coaching can help (E) coachees say help the coachee get his thoughts organized to know what they want to do. The Slavs have an expression that puts this same idea in another way: Prvo ispeci pa posle reci, which means, "First bake it. Then serve it." A coach can instruct the (E) coachee to —whenever they have a new idea—write it down and file it in a folder called "Ideas," and to review this folder only when needed for action. Upon later review, the (E) might more easily determine which ideas were silly or not a high priority. Furthermore, the coach might encourage the (E) to classify the ideas in the folder into different categories (e.g., health, well-being, hobbies, relationships, family, career), to be handled either in one-on-one coaching or through self-coaching (whichever makes the most sense).

"People just don't get it. They don't understand."

A common complaint of (E) coachees is that the people in their lives don't understand them.

It's possible that the disagreements and misunderstandings they think they're hearing from others are really coming from inside themselves.

(E)s need to learn to listen to themselves. They might be the first to disagree with what they have just said.

When we coach the (E)s we help them to become aware of what they want before they say what they don't want. To reach agreement with others, they must first agree with themselves.

We encourage them to slow down, to make sure they understand what they themselves have just said. As an exercise, we ask them to write their ideas down, then read what they wrote. If they agree with what they've written, and it is plausible and implementable, they can then communicate it.

If, however, they need to change what they wrote, that means they did not understand themselves either. Their frustration and hostility toward others ("Why don't they understand?") is misplaced. In reality, they are annoyed at themselves for not knowing what they themselves want!

To develop this awareness, we ask the (E) to always carry a pad and pen with them—to write down their ideas and clarify them for themselves before they communicate them to others.

> *"A fish dies through its mouth." (Brazilian saying)*
>
> *"In a closed mouth, a fly does not get in." (Spanish Sephardic saying)*
>
> *"Speech is silver, silence is golden." (Hebrew saying)*
>
> *"Life and death are in the power of the tongue." (Talmud)*

There are aphorisms in many languages that all mean the same thing: "Be careful what you say."

"There is always a better option. Let's improve some more!"

Sometimes (E) coachees will try to improve and improve and improve, until the cost of the improvement exceeds its value, making the situation worse, not better. At a certain point, they have to learn to say, "It's good enough. Stop!"

In a coaching process, this can sabotage execution and results, making the (E) work on something but never finishing it, because they're always trying to change because they have another idea which they believe it to be a better idea assuming that different is always better.

Through their quest for imaginary perfection, hardly ever well defined and finalized, (E)s can ruin their own chances of implementing a good enough solution. Less happens, rather than more.

Whether the decision is about how to decorate (or redecorate) their home, or what gym membership to obtain, or anything else in their personal or professional lives, (E)s tend to fall into this trap.

So, how do they learn to stop themselves from continuously "improving"?

First, we encourage them to set a deadline by which they must arrive at a finalization, and also to not procrastinate because they believe they might have a better idea tomorrow. We use their bias multiple to help them set the deadline.

We as coaches insist they set up a deadline by when the decision is final (when the deadline arrives, if there is no finalization, the latest illumination must automatically become the finalization), and if it is to be changed it cannot be changed for a certain period of time, in order to give the decision a chance to work.

"Save me the details."

One of the main benefits of coaching is the clarification of the coachee's mind through the process. Clarity in coaching is achieved through attention to detail. But (E)s look at the big picture: the horizon, the excitement, the potential, the opportunities.

Typically, (E)s only enjoy dealing with the first fifty percent of the coaching process: they get excited by the generating of possibilities and the brainstorming of options. They'd prefer, however, to skip the other fifty percent: working through the process and executing their goals (especially when this involves second-order change). But the set-up phase (the first fifty percent) of the process is not enough to achieve the desired results. As Thomas Edison once said, "Genius is one percent inspiration, ninety-nine percent perspiration."

In other words, talent isn't enough. Good ideas aren't enough. Coaching is not "talk therapy." The focus is on obtaining concrete, measurable results and improvements. So it's important to focus not only on a solution but also on the means necessary to implement that solution. The full coaching process involves not only what and why, but how and who.

The key is to help the coachee stay consistent and not abandon the coaching process when the going gets boring. So we coach them to create an action plan with detailed steps that show how to implement the idea.

It has been said that "the road to Hell is paved with good intentions." In other words, it is not the goal itself but the small details that make or break the process.

The general concept is important—very important—but how it is translated into operative details is what really counts. (E)s must learn to go through the hell of details to reach the heaven of a workable solution.

"All of these options look the same."

(E) coachees paint with a wide brush. They tend to generalize and exaggerate what they know. They're hyperbolic: They love words like "never," "always," "everything." They find it difficult to interest themselves in small distinctions.

For an extreme (E) there are no nuances, there is no granularity. If, during the coaching process, they discuss alternative A, and the coach suggests alternative B, an (E) will decide, "Both of them are no good."

"Why?"
"Because they are the same."

"But they are not the same," the coach might say. "They're different. The difference is a small one, but they are different."

The (E) will insist: "They are the same." The (E) is looking at the big picture, and in the big picture small differences do not matter.

Often in coaching very small changes are what unlock tremendous progress. The tiniest little calibrations are what may solve the problem. As a matter of fact, in my coaching practice I work hard to make the smallest change necessary to solve a problem. I sometimes think of myself as a cosmetic surgeon. Can you imagine what would happen if clients came out of my treatment and people hardly recognized them? Ideally, people should not even realize there was a surgery; the person just looks better or younger, and people do not know why.

But when small changes are suggested, I am told—typically by an (E)—"No, I've tried that before and it didn't work." And it may be true that they tried something similar, but it was not the same.

Still, they will tell me, "It's more or less the same."

So I give them an analogy: "Let's assume your car is not working properly. You take it to the garage, and the mechanic reconnects one wire, that's all. This solves the problem. When you look at the car, it looks the same except for one little wire that is now correctly connected. So it is similar, but at the same time, it is a different car, because it works! One little variable can make all the difference."

In medical diagnoses, one symptom can be the difference between disease A and disease B.

So we help the (E) learn not to generalize unnecessarily—to pay attention to the details, and too focus—in order to see the differences and the similarities.

"Why not use one single coaching process for a large number of goals?"

(E)s tend to believe that they can go on to achieve a multiplicity of goals in one single coaching process. When asked what are seeking coaching for, they may say, "Just to lose weight." But then it will come out that the coachee's spouse does all of the cooking, and they fight a lot over food. The (E) will want to work on this issue too.—and also some other issues, in fact, quite a few.

Sometimes these "additionals" will appear under the guise of "Can I ask you a simple question, unrelated to our main goal?" And it is soon discovered that the issue is not "simple" at all.

So, in the beginning, we first ask them what it is they want to work on. And then we add: "Good. Great. Now let's identify which of these issues are needed right now, and which would be nice to accomplish but they can wait for a while, and which cannot be worked on right now because they are more complex and deserve separate treatment."

And continue to guide them: "Now, let's give each item on the 'need right now list' a priority."

As we work with them to categorize their lists, we help them to realize that they cannot have "everything" right now, that not everything is of equal importance, and that not everything will be handled (or "coached") in the same way. (E)s have lots of difficulty with deciding what not to do, because they can't decide why not to do it. If they prioritize by deciding only what to do, they might end up with so many priorities that few if any get carried out. What's more, they also can't imagine that a separate approach might be needed and even beneficial to different types of issues.

HOW TO COACH THE (I) STYLE

First, create rapport: match the (I)'s personality frequency

In order to create rapport with an (I)-style coachee, you need to take into account their interpersonal and relational manner. To relate best to this style, follow these guidelines:

- To match their (I) language, you must remain people oriented. And show that you really care.
- Don't get right to business. Spend a few minutes asking them about their week. Be personal. That's how you create a relationship with them. This shows them you care. This shows them you are coming from the heart. Even in a business setting or if you are doing executive coaching with them—be personal.
- Match the tempo of the conversation to theirs—especially if you are a (P) or an (E) type. (I)s usually speak slowly.
- A very important tip: Never rush them. To challenge them to step out of their comfort zone, you need to do so slowly and smoothly. Never too drastic, never asking them to take too big of a step. You need to keep the flow going, the good vibes. This doesn't mean that there is no agenda or structure to the coaching process. What it means is: Don't come across too bossy or too pushy. Keep it friendly. And stay accessible to them. They move slowly and then suddenly make big jumps, so be patient. If you see that they talk a lot but actually do very little, gently encourage them to take little steps so as to achieve some progress.
- Make sure you don't go overboard with academic, intellectual, or mental energy. Don't overanalyze things. Don't go too much into your own head, or become too systematic.

They will perceive you as cold. It's ok to analyze and use systems, but stay balanced, never lose contact with your heart.

The diagnosis stage with an (I) style

Because of their interpersonal and relational orientation, (I)s can spend an inordinate amount of time dealing with the people aspect of any problem.

Diagnosing the coaching problem with an (I) requires mainly a good analysis of the (P), (A), and (E) aspects of the challenge, because an (I) will naturally tend to view most problems from the people side.

Setting coaching goals with the (I) style

In coaching, when the time comes for setting goals, we need to remember that (I)s are relational beings. Their quest for consensus and harmony is what drives them. They are convinced that if other people are ok, they are going to be ok too.

Thus, the main challenge when setting goals with them, is to help them connect with what they really want and need.

It's important that the coach helps them to stop worrying about what people will say regarding the (I)'s coaching goal, or that the caoching goal is not theirs but what people told them they should do and they now comply. Someone might say something no matter what the (I) does. There will be situations in the (I)'s life that may require that they jump into the fray and take immediate action without waiting for agreement. **They will have to decide on their own what they need.** It's good to seek out other's opinions, but a person also needs to think independently.

The values of (I) people: what's important to the (I) coachee

In a coaching process with an (I) coachee it's important to always remember their values—the issues and principles that are important to them, that are central in their life.

Here is a list of their toward values (the things they most seek to achieve):

consensus, harmony, tolerance, patience, tact, diplomacy

Here is a list of the things they try to avoid:

insensitivity, conflict, coldness, disharmony, impatience, rudeness

The Limiting Beliefs of the (I) coachee: and the lenses through which they see the world

The (I) mindset is sustained by a series of limiting beliefs. In coaching we bring awareness to these beliefs. Following are some of the most crippling beliefs of the (I) personality:

"Disagreements really annoy me."

An (I) coachee may come to the coaching session complaining about a friend. "He calls me every night and sometimes I am very tired and don't want to talk. But somehow, I stay on the phone, waiting for him to finish and hang up." If the coach asks, "What prevents you from ending the conversation yourself and hanging up?" the answer may be, "I don't want to offend my friend. I don't want to anger him or get into a disagreement with him."

> *"Nothing is more obstinate than a fashionable consensus."* —Margaret Thatcher

(I)s like harmony and easy-flowing discussion. If there is a disagreement, especially a noisy one, they might interpret it as intolerable and try to stop it. Their main fear is that the disagreement will spiral out of control, to the point where their ability to achieve harmony—where they feel comfortable—will be overwhelmed.

But a noisy disagreement just means that there's a lot of emotion and many different opinions. It doesn't necessarily mean the conversation is heading out of control.

We encourage the (I) to not be afraid of heated and emotional discussions, and also encourage them to not push their disagreements under the rug. Coach should teach the coachee the Adizes rules of how to integrate a team: there must be rules to practice mutual respect, no interpuptions, no changing the subject discussed till it is closed, not raising voices, no offensive language ... With rules and protocols based on mutual respect, recognizing each others right to think differently, the disagreements can be civilized and acceptabe by the (I) style.

"Taking into account what people are feeling is always an imperative."

An (I) pays less attention to what people say than to how they feel about what they say. Feelings are important, but what is more important is what is causing those feelings: the problem itself. For a little while at least, in the interest of getting what they want, (I)s need to be able to hear what is being said and simultaneously ignore the subtext.

"It's always good to consult with friends before making a decision."

(I)s may complicate the coaching process by working with the coach on a subject, and in between sessions go "opinion shopping," consulting with their friends about the work they are doing with the coach. The problem is that friend #1 may coincide with the coach, but friend #2 may have a different opinion, and friend #3 may contradict what friends #2 and #1 have said. By the end of this, the (I) coachee may come back to the coach, asking to "solve" and reconcile this multiplicity of opinions—extremely confused by it all.

This presents a unique learning opportunity for the (I): that bad decisions can be made by consensus. And that the quality of a decision is not a function of how many people agree with it; it's a function of how successfully it moves the (I) forward on their coaching goals. The goal of .the process is for the coachee to discover for himslef what is it that he wants independently of what others want him to want. To emancipate his will from being the response to the will of others.

"Let's postpone the decision until there is a complete consensus."

Sometimes in coaching, the (I)s will repeatedly postpone a decision until there is a complete consensus from other people.

(I)s need to learn to make a distinction between a total consensus and a workable consensus. A workable consensus is an agreement that the critical people have bought into and that can safely be implemented.

Whether at home or at work, it's important that (I) coachees understand that there is a price to procrastination, and value in a decision made in a timely manner. They need to be reminded that a decision is rendered successful by its results, not by how many people agree with it.

A perfect consensus is a rare and wonderful thing, but it is not always necessary when making and implementing a decision. Is the (I) overweight but the spouse refuses to cooperate and clear all of the junk food out of the kitchen? It's not possible sometimes to wait until everybody agrees, to start with a plan.

Are these other people critical for the implementation? If yes, the (I) will have to convince them or accommodate them. If the (I) can do the diet anyways, then the (I) heard them out, made the decision; and it's time to move on.

"Rejection is a terrible thing."

> *"Oh, I've always been very ...emotional. 'Hypersensitive' is what they call it, I think."* —Aurora (Norwegian musician)

(I)s, like (E)s, do not like conflict. A strong coach, who challenges (I)s to get out of their comfort zone, can be perceived as rejecting them.

But conflicts can be extremely helpful in filling out a picture and seeing all the dimensions of a problem. We help the (I)s remember that a challenge, and even a conflict, can be an opportunity to learn. A challenge should not be taken as a personal rejection.

"I feel I need to please them."

> *"There just isn't any pleasing some people. The trick is to stop trying."* —Robert Mitchum

A common complaint from (I) coachees is feeling overwhelmed by other people's agendas and demands. As we saw above in "Setting coaching goals with the (I) coachee", with the (I) commonly disconnects from their own needs, and therefore, needs to learn how to reconnect with what they really want. But there is another angle to this: what other people want, is not necessarily what needs to change.

For instance, parents are aware of what their kids want, but they cannot always give them what they want—and sometimes tough love is appropriate. The parents love their kids, they care for them, but at the same time they decide what they can and can't have.

As coaches, we need to help (I)s realize that although they are good listeners, and they care about what others want and need, in their own lives they need to make decisions for themselves, based on their own wants and needs. Because every person in the (I)'s life may not be exactly aligned with their interests, or know what is best for them.

Part 5:

For certified coaches of other approaches

If you are a certified coach, you'll find it very useful to translate many of your existing coaching tools into Adizes terms, to add them depth and powerful applications.

As an example, let's analyze the GROW model—one of the most widely accepted coaching methods—which emerged in the United Kingdom in the late 1980s, and has been used extensively in life and corporate coaching.

GROW is an acronym for:

- G (GOAL): The goal is the end point, where the coachee wants to be. It has to be defined in such a way that, when it's achieved, it is very clear to the client.
- R (REALITY): The client's current reality, where they are now. From here, it is determined how far they are from their goal, and what issues and challenges exist.

- O (OPTIONS): The client needs to find ways to: 1. deal with any obstacles 2. make progress.
- W (WAY FORWARD): The client's options are converted into action steps, which they then follow to their goal. The "W" of GROW may also stand for: when, by whom, and will (the client's intention/commitment) to follow through.

Coaches using GROW typically follow the exact sequence of the letters: First, they set the goal, then they check the current reality and determine the gap between it and the client's goal, then they look for options, and finally they create an action plan.

As you may have noticed in Part 3 of this book, in Adizes we don't start the sequence in setting the "goal" as in GROW. Why? Because many times we know what we want to achieve, and we can clearly articulate our goal, yet for some reason, we end up frustrated because we are not able to implement the solution we want.

Notice how the sequence that has been followed here is want => is => should. What you want, followed by what is, and then by what you should have or do.

The problem with this commonly used sequence is that energy is fixed at any point in time. And in the sequence want => is => should, there is a "leak" somewhere that robs the solution of energy. This can cause us to end up more frustrated with our solution than with the problem.

Where is the leak?

We didn't start the whole process with the "is," the current reality. We didn't give ourselves enough time to fully analyze and understand the "is." As we deliberate what we "should" do, and what we "want," the "is" might get lost and little or no attention is given to it. Deep inside our conscience there are doubts as to what we can do and if this is the real problem and thus if it's the right solution.

In Adizes, the self-coaching process starts with the "is" imperative, that is, a deep assessment of your present reality. We work to uncover what is really going on. We guide our coachees to admit what the problem is. They confess it openly and clearly. By diagnosing their own problem, they free their fixed energy, which puts them in a place to be able to (eventually) solve their problem. When you admit your reality "as is," you stop denying it. This frees all the energy that was stuck while you were busy fighting reality.

The mistake is to start with the want, not giving enough attention to the is—or worse, starting with what you should do, ignoring the reality.

Imagine an architect that designs a house based in the should—the principles of architectural design—but ignores where the building is located, and what the client really wants.

When solving a problem never start with what you want. Start with what is going on. Get anchored in reality. Then ask yourself what you want in light of that reality, and subsequently ask yourself what you should do to change the reality you do not want. If you start from want and then go to is, your want is based not on reality but might be on adream like desire whcih has zero chance to be reached and than when you bring the is reality to be analyzed the disparity between the dreaml like want and the rude reality can be such the coachee instead of feeling emoowered feels disemooweredwhich is not constructive for coahing for results.

> *IS => WANT => SHOULD => new IS*

Once you have honestly assessed your reality, which was presented above in how to diagnose the problem, you can now ask what is it that you want. Now a gap was created, between what is (the reality, your point A) and where you want to get (your goal, point B). This gap is frustrating, and all energy can be now focused on what you should do.

There are no subsequent chapter. The book doesnot end well.

In subsequent chapters we will discuss how to design the task that needs to be done and choose the desired criteria for a solution.

Epilogue

Self-coaching and coaching others—the foundations for our growth and contribution to others—are both a science and an art, and throughout this book we learned how to achieve these, step-by-step, with the Adizes Systemic Coaching Methodology. Grounded on over fifty years of field research, the Adizes Methodology is a major departure from traditional coaching methods, which often fall into the "one size fits all" trap as they don't distinguish personality styles, assuming that what works in coaching one person will also work for another. In addition, the Adizes techniques help individuals to systematically become more flexible and well-balanced, as well as more effective and efficient, in both the short and long run. Not by changing their style but by developing the roles that are missing - taking into account the lifecycle location - to bring about personal, internal integration that leads to a more externally integrated and functional human being.

A famous saying in air travel is "put on your oxygen mask first," because you must prioritize self-care before you can help others. In the same fashion, it's only after we learned in Part 3 how to do self-coaching that we moved into how to coach others in Part 4. It's a basic Adizes tenet that only when you are able to take care of your own internal disintegration, and become more whole as a human being, are you able to help others. If you are "not together," you do not have the energy that is required to coach others. The way to make your coaching powerful is to coach yourself first.

With some issues in your life you will be able to apply the self-coaching protocols for first-order change smoothly and quickly. You'll find other, more complex problems to be like a tangled ball of string. How will you untie it? You have learned how to carefully apply the second-order change protocols. You have learned how to think about interdependencies and boundaries. You have learned to pull gently from one string until there is resistance. You have learned to loosen the string that is obstructing the first one. You have also learned to return to the first string and continue loosening, until progress is made.

So be patient. And remember it's a long journey ahead, so do the work and don't beat yourself up too much when things don't turn out exactly as planned. When you see slow progress, hit a plateau, or make no progress at all, do not give up, know that it's time for corrective action. Stay in learning mode. If you follow the protocols in this book, you'll see that some results appear quickly while others take more time, but you will always be gaining in process. That's guaranteed. You will be conditioning yourself for a more integrated, happier, and healthier life.

May these teachings help you become aligned and integrate yourself, so that through your coaching you can be a light that shines love and integration in the world. And I hope one day to hear about your success. Please share with me any insights, questions, or feedback on this book at ichak@adizes.com.

With all my blessings,

Dr. Ichak Adizes

About the Author

For more than fifty years, Dr. Ichak Kalderon Adizes has developed, tested, and documented the proprietary methodology that bears his name. The Adizes Symbergetic Methodology is used to manage and lead change for exceptional results, effectively and efficiently, and without destructive conflict. *Leadership Excellence Magazine* named Dr. Adizes one of the "Top Thirty Thought Leaders on Leadership," and PRovoke Media (formerly The Holmes Report) named him one of the "Best Communicators Among World Leaders" in 2017 — alongside Pope Francis, Angela Merkel, and the Dalai Lama.

In 2019, in recognition of his contributions to management theory and practice, Dr. Adizes received a Lifetime Achievement Award from the International Academy of Management. He has also been awarded twenty-one honorary doctorates from universities in eleven countries.

Dr. Adizes is a former tenured faculty member at UCLA. He has taught as a visiting professor at Stanford University, Tel Aviv University, and Hebrew University, and as a lecturer with the Columbia

University Executive Program. He has served as dean of the Adizes Graduate School for the Study of Organizational Therapy and Collaborative Leadership and was an academic advisor to the International School of Management for the Academy of National Economy of the Russian Federation.

He is the founder of the Adizes Institute, an international change-management company based in Santa Barbara, California, that delivers the Adizes Program for Symbergetic change management to clients in the public and private sectors. In addition to advising prime ministers and cabinet-level officers across the world, Dr. Adizes has delivered the Adizes program to a wide variety of companies ranging from start-ups to members of the Fortune 100.

Dr. Adizes lectures in four languages and has appeared before well over two hundred and fifty thousand senior-level executives in more than fifty-two countries, and several million over the Internet. His book *Managing Corporate Lifecycles* was named one of the "Ten Best Business Books" by *Library Journal*. He is an international bestseller and has published twenty-eight books, translated into a combined total of thirty-six languages.

Dr. Adizes is married with six grown children. Living in Santa Barbara, California, he loves to play the accordion, and practices yoga and Heartfulness meditation.

BOOKS BY THE AUTHOR

Publications.Adizes.com

1. Adizes, I. *The Power of Collaborative Leadership*. Forthcoming, 2023.
2. Adizes, I. *Systemic Coaching*. Forthcoming, 2023.
3. Adizes, I. *The Accordion Player: My Journey from Fear to Love*. Forthcoming, 2023.
4. Adizes, I. *What Matters in Life*. Forthcoming, 2023.
5. Adizes, I. *Insights On Socio-Political Issues: Volume III*. Santa Barbara, CA: Adizes Institute Publications, 2019.
6. Adizes, I. *Insights on Personal Growth: Volume III*. Santa Barbara, CA: Adizes Institute Publications, 2019.
7. Adizes, I. *Insights on Management: Volume III*. Santa Barbara, CA: Adizes Institute Publications, 2018.
8. Adizes, I., with Yechezkel and Ruth Madanes. *The Power of Opposites*. Santa Barbara, CA: Adizes Institute Publications, 2015.
9. Adizes, I. *Mastering Change*. Santa Barbara, CA: Adizes Institute Publications, 1992. Revised edition, Adizes Institute Publications, 2015.
10. Adizes, I. *Insights on Management: Volume II*. Santa Barbara, CA: Adizes Institute Publications, 2014.
11. Adizes, I. *Insights on Personal Growth: Volume II*. Santa Barbara, CA: Adizes Institute Publications, 2014.
12. Adizes, I. *Insights on Policy Issues: Volume II*. Santa Barbara, CA: Adizes Institute Publications, 2014.
13. Adizes, I. *Food for Thought: On What Counts in Life*. Santa Barbara, CA: Adizes Institute Publications, 2012.
14. Adizes, I. *Food for Thought: On Change and Leadership*. Santa Barbara, CA: Adizes Institute Publications, 2012.

15. Adizes, I. *Food for Thought: On Management.* Santa Barbara, CA: Adizes Institute Publications, 2012.

16. Adizes, I. *Insights on Management: Volume I.* Santa Barbara, CA: Adizes Institute Publications, 2011.

17. Adizes, I. *Insights on Personal Growth: Volume I.* Santa Barbara, CA: Adizes Institute Publications, 2011.

18. Adizes, I. *Insights on Policy: Volume I.* Santa Barbara, CA: Adizes Institute Publications, 2011.

19. Adizes, I. *How to Manage in Times of Crisis (And How to Avoid a Crisis in the First Place).* Santa Barbara, CA: Adizes Institute Publications, 2009.

20. Adizes, I. *Leading the Leaders: How to Enrich Your Style of Management and Handle People Whose Style Is Different from Yours.* Santa Barbara, CA: Adizes Institute Publications, 2004.

21. Adizes, I. *Management/Mismanagement Styles: How to Identify a Style and What to Do About It.* Santa Barbara, CA: Adizes Institute Publications, 2004.

22. Adizes I. *Corporate Lifecycles: How Organizations Grow, Age, and Die.* Initial publication by Prentice Hall, 1990. Reprint, Santa Barbara, CA: Adizes Institute Publications. New revised edition: *Managing Corporate Lifecycles: Complete Volume* or *Volume 1 and Volume 2*, Santa Barbara, CA: Adizes Institute Publications, 2004.

23. Adizes, I. *The Ideal Executive: Why You Cannot Be One and What to Do About It.* Santa Barbara, CA: Adizes Institute Publications, 2004.

24. Adizes, I. *Conversations with CEOs.* Santa Barbara, CA: Adizes Institute Publications, 2004.

25. Adizes, I. *The Pursuit of Prime.* Santa Monica, CA: Knowledge Exchange, 1996. Reprint, Santa Barbara, CA: Adizes Institute Publications.

26. Adizes, I. *How to Solve the Mismanagement Crisis*. Homewood, IL: Dow Jones/ Irwin, 1985. Reprint, Santa Barbara, CA: Adizes Institute Publications.

27. Adizes, I., and E. Mann Borgese, eds., *Self-Management: New Dimensions to Democracy*. Santa Barbara, CA: ABC-CLIO, 1975. Reprint, Santa Barbara, CA: Adizes Institute Publications.

28. Adizes, I. *Industrial Democracy: Yugoslav Style*. New York Free Press, 1971. Reprint, Santa Barbara, CA: Adizes Institute Publications.

VIDEOS BY THE AUTHOR

https://www.youtube.com/c/adizesofficial/
https://www.youtube.com/c/DrIchakAdizes-channel/

WEBSITES

https://www.ichakadizes.com/
https://adizes.com/

THE ADIZES® SYMBERGETIC™ METHODOLOGY FOR MANAGING CHANGE

This theory and its protocols on how to manage change with any system — an individual, a marriage, a for profit or nonprofit company, and society — has been tested successfully for over fifty years in over fifty countries. It is transferable and teachable, and as of 2022 there are over seventy Certified Associates worldwide who practice and teach this methodology through the Adizes institute in their country. For more info, see www.adizes.com.

THE ADIZES INSTITUTE

Through its ten offices, the institute serves companies worldwide to manage change. Its services encompass corporate transformation to reach Prime, online leadership training, digital support apps, executive search, C-level coaching, family coaching, training and certification of organizational symbergists (those that teach and practice the methodology), and the Adizes Graduate School, whose purpose is to train university faculty in the methodology and to support scientific research.

www.ingramcontent.com/pod-product-compliance
Lightning Source LLC
Chambersburg PA
CBHW060340170426
43202CB00014B/2826